This edition first published in the UK in 2005 by
Green Umbrella Publishing

Printed and bound in Italy

ISBN 1-905009-97-6

Contents

THE LORD'S TAVERNERS

Foreword

Message from the president of The Lord's Taverners

Above
Those were the days! John Emburey and me on England's victorious Ashes tour of 1986/87.

I am delighted to be asked to write the foreword to this excellent account of our wonderful Ashes victory by my old friends Ralph Dellor and Stephen Lamb. Keen students of the game will doubtless be hoping for more than one 2005 Ashes book in their Christmas stockings. This one is an absolute must.

Besides the anticipation of an historic victory, around 4pm on Monday 12 September 2005 was a moment of enormous relief for me personally. With a draw in the Oval Test match now assured I was not only about to be relieved, after nearly 19 years, of the tag of being the last England captain to win the Ashes, but I was also absolved from having Rod Marsh shave off my beard and moustache. Rod was not so lucky!

Let me tell you how this came about. As president of the Lord's Taverners I have been letting myself in for all manner of fundraising ventures in the past two years. Their latest jape, called "The Tashes", was a bet, from which the charity would benefit, between Rod and myself on who would win the Ashes. England's victory was doubly beneficial for the charity because our friendly bookmakers had naturally made Australia favourites at the beginning of the summer. So an England win was a bonanza for the charity and also allowed me to get to work on Rod's 'tache as dusk was falling at the Oval on that never to be forgotten day.

It is good to be involved once again with Ralph and Stephen and their company, Sportsline Media Limited. They are both outstanding cricket journalists and their knowledge shines forth in this book. They capture the tension of the Tests so well. For me, some of the key moments were literally unwatchable. If I didn't quite hide behind my sofa, I have to admit that the tension that last morning at Edgbaston was more than I could take. As an Australian win looked increasingly on the cards, I ran for the cover of my car and drove home, only just being brave enough to turn on Test Match Special for those last pulsating few minutes.

Above
What can I say!?
The Tashes!!

What would have happened if Australia had edged home doesn't bear thinking about. Instead our summer was transformed.

I suppose the other aspect that will long live in the memory was the manner in which the series was played – tough as they come but with great camaraderie and respect between the teams. If the image of Freddie Flintoff consoling Brett Lee will be the abiding memory, my own highlight was at the Oval. Kevin Pietersen had just been bowled by Glenn McGrath after an innings of staggering power that had literally saved England. Two hours earlier Shane Warne had dropped Pietersen at first slip – by his standards a pretty regulation catch. Yet here was Warne, racing up from the boundary at the far end of the ground, to congratulate his Hampshire colleague as he returned to the pavilion.

They will be telling their grandchildren about these moments for as long as the game of cricket is played. And you can enjoy them again and again if you manage to lay your hands on this book before it is sold out!

Mike Gatting OBE

Introduction

NEVER has an Ashes series been anticipated more keenly; never has the cricketing nation had to wait so long into the season to savour the considerable delights it had to offer when it eventually arrived.

England had already had to endure 16 long years of what was quite often humiliation since their captain had last enjoyed the sensation of holding the urn. That was Mike Gatting after the 1986/87 series in Australia,

Below
Ashes flashback – Tim Zoehrer is caught by Bill Athey at short leg during England's last series victory in 1986-87.

with a side that been labelled as no-hopers at the outset. One newspaper correspondent had famously said after a tour match defeat that there were “only three things wrong with this English side: they can’t bat, they can’t bowl and they can’t field.” They proceeded to win everything in sight.

There were rather higher hopes of the 2005 England team because they entered the series with a fine track record. They had comprehensively beaten West Indies away, then New Zealand and West Indies at home. They had gone to South Africa and won. That was pedigree form.

Above
England celebrate the fall of another Australian wicket during the 1986-87 series.

Right
Mike Gatting and his victorious team. It was to be 19 years before England’s Ashes champagne flowed again.

Above
Ian Bell progresses towards his maiden Test century against Bangladesh at Chester-le-Street.

In the days of two series summers, the England and Wales Cricket Board had decided that before the Ashes began, there would be no end of build-up matches to whet the appetite – or perhaps sate it.

The series against Bangladesh was a useful way for the England players to get into the mood for Test cricket and work rustiness out of the system. That appeared much needed during the first Test at Lord's where the bowling was wayward on the first morning until the radar was adjusted and Bangladesh were swept away by an innings and 261 runs. It was much the same story at Chester-le-Street for the second Test, where it was an innings and 27 runs but the game occupied even less time on the third morning.

The Twenty20 international gave the one-day squad an idea of what it was like to thump the Australians comprehensively: not many English players had experienced that feeling. England scored 179 for eight from their 20 overs, while Australia managed only 79 in 14.3 overs to lose by a satisfyingly symmetrical 100 runs.

"Ah yes," was the cry, "but they were not taking it seriously; it was only a bit of fun."

It was not much fun for the Australians when they somewhat arrogantly decided to bat in the first match of the NatWest Series against Bangladesh in Cardiff. They no doubt intended to post a massive total and then bowl Bangladesh out cheaply to bolster confidence. They had just lost a tour match against Somerset by four wickets, so confidence could have done with bolstering, but Bangladesh kept the Australian total down to 249 for five

Right
Mohammad Ashraful of Bangladesh celebrating his match-winning century against Australia in Cardiff.

in 50 overs and proceeded to knock off the runs with five wickets and four balls in hand.

These Australians were shown to be human and not unbeatable, as England demonstrated yet again the next day in Bristol. Inspired by Kevin Pietersen – not for the last time in this momentous summer – England won by three wickets.

Australia won the next meeting quite comfortably, honours were even when the weather washed out the next group match, while the final at Lord's gave heart to those who had forecast a close tussle all summer. It ended in a tie when Ashley Giles scrambled two leg byes off the last ball. Like Pietersen, he was to play a not insignificant part with the bat at the other, climactic, end of the summer.

The cricket world was now eager for the Ashes to begin, with the sides obviously so evenly matched. Yet there was still the NatWest Challenge to be completed. Apart from filling the coffers, there was little justification for this additional delay before the main event. When Australia won the series two-one, there was even more criticism of the impostor in the fixture list.

At last, the sides could put away their coloured clothing; they could change their personnel from the one-

Above
Michael Vaughan and Ricky Ponting share the NatWest Series trophy after the final ended in a tie.

In Affectionate Remembrance
OF
ENGLISH CRICKET,
WHICH DIED AT THE OVAL
ON
29th AUGUST, 1882,
Deeply lamented by a large circle of sorrowing friends and acquaintances.

R. I. P.

N.B.—The body will be cremated and the ashes taken to Australia.

Above
The Sporting Times obituary on the death of English cricket which appeared after England lost the 1882 Test Match against Australia.

Right
The original Ashes urn, now on permanent display in the museum at Lord's Cricket Ground.

day to Test squads; they could forget all about substitutes (of the batting and bowling varieties at least, and until Ricky Ponting made a bit of a prat of himself) and power plays, and get on with the real business of the summer, the battle for the Ashes.

England had enjoyed a recent run of success in Test cricket while Australia enjoyed an air of invincibility stretching back for years. In one-day cricket England had shown that they could look the old enemy in the eye and not flinch. How would it be in Test cricket? The answer was that these two evenly-matched sides would provide a feast of entertainment, some technical deficiencies, especially in the field, some memorable cricket and some of the most exciting contests since the Ashes first came into existence in 1882.

That year, the tension was such at the Oval that one spectator allegedly chewed through his umbrella handle and another died of a haemorrhage despite the ministrations of a certain doctor present on the ground, by the name of W.G. Grace. England's defeat in that match gave rise to the mock obituary in the Sporting Times, and the following winter the actual trophy came into existence. England came back from a first Test defeat to win the series two-one and regain the Ashes.

No umbrella handles were reported to be ruined during the Oval Test of 2005, while England did come back from a heavy defeat in the first Test to regain the Ashes by a two-one margin. If history did not actually repeat itself, there were echoes of the past by the end of the summer. But by then, a series of unrelenting vitality confined admirably within the spirit of cricket had entertained everybody like no other in modern times.

FULLER'S LONDON PRIDE
European Law Firm
TOYOTA Avensis
NatWest
25 Years In Cricket

Chapter One

Lord's

EVEN the most optimistic followers of English cricket could hardly believe their eyes, but it was true. It had to be, because it was there, emblazoned on the Lord's scoreboard. Australia 190 all out. One-day internationals had their place and the Twenty20 contest had been a pleasing diversion, but this was Test cricket and, for once, all the hyperbole that had preceded it proved to have solid foundations.

Of course, English euphoria could not last as Glenn McGrath had to ruin everything by claiming his place in history, but even when that same scoreboard showed England 92 for seven at close of play, there was a sense that this had been a special day in the history of the Ashes. As the match and the series unfolded, it was shown that the first day of the first Test had set the tone for the entire Ashes series of 2005.

When Australia won the toss and elected to bat, most of the capacity crowd thronging the ground appeared resigned to watching the England bowlers toiling and the fielders chasing leather to all parts of London NW8.

Below
The Ashes get under way as Stephen Harmison of England bowls the first ball to Justin Langer of Australia on day one of the first Test.

Above
Matthew Hoggard celebrates taking the wicket of Matthew Hayden.

As the eighth over was about to be completed with the score on 35, there was little to suggest anything other than the usual pattern for England v Australia. Then Matthew Hoggard bowled Matthew Hayden and the series was really under way.

Justin Langer hung around before Andrew Flintoff got him, Ricky Ponting had already fallen to Stephen Harmison while Damien Martyn and Michael Clarke both went to Simon Jones before the innings was 22 overs old and with only 87 runs on the board. Ten more runs were added before lunch, but whatever was served up in those members' hampers behind the pavilion, and whatever was decanted to wash it down, nothing could compare with the fare that was being served up out on the field. It was heady stuff.

Adam Gilchrist threatened to do what he does best with some dashing strokes producing six boundaries before Flintoff began what was, for him, a happy knack of trapping the Australian wicket-keeper from round the wicket. So often in the past we had seen the English attack disciplined and penetrative in the early stages; just as often we had seen late resistance from the Australian lower order to turn a sub-standard total into one of annoying respectability. This time it was different.

Above
Harmison celebrates with his team mates after taking the final wicket of Jason Gillespie.

Instead of offering irritating defiance, the tail was swept away by the venomous bowling of Harmison. He had begun by taking the first over for the first time in his Test career, and made an impression by striking Langer painfully on the elbow with his second ball. More significantly, Ponting had taken a blow on the helmet from a Harmison delivery which pressed the grille into his cheek, causing a wound which required stitches and left Australia's captain permanently battle-scarred. Now he took the last four wickets that fell for the addition of only 15 runs in four overs for England to claim the ascendancy for the first time in the series. The Australian batsmen were shocked by Harmison, who finished with five

for 43, while the other three bowlers used had all made telling contributions.

With each wicket that had fallen, the buzz of excited chatter that is normal for Lord's on the first day of a Test had erupted into a roar of approval. Much had been made of the fact that it was unusual for the first Ashes clash to be scheduled for Lord's and not the second, as is traditional. Few of the reasons given carried much conviction for, surely, all other considerations should have been put aside for a match of such magnitude?

The general feeling was that Edgbaston would have provided a more suitable venue for the first Test because Lord's tended to inspire visiting sides, especially Australian ones, to greater heights, while the crowds in Birmingham were likely to be more raucously patriotic. Perhaps they would, but with extra seating erected especially for the occasion, there was no shortage of vocal support in appreciation of England's efforts that first day. Even normally staid MCC members were showing a degree of excitement and agitation not usually associated with the venue. It was not to last.

McGrath had started the match with much publicity centred on the fact that he needed one wicket to reach 500 in Test cricket. As soon as the tour schedule was announced, he began fuelling the verbal posturing by nominating Marcus Trescothick as his 500th victim in his first over at Lord's. While McGrath nominated the right batsman, the timing of his prophecy failed to live up to Muhammad Ali-like accuracy.

Right
McGrath salutes the crowd after taking the wicket of Trescothick – his 500th in Test cricket.

The wicket did not materialise until the first ball after tea when Trescothick edged to Langer at slip and McGrath donned a special pair of boots embroidered with a 500 motif in gold. They did not weigh too heavily on his feet or his reputation, for with the first ball of his ninth over he took his own tally of victims to 504 and had England

had been man of the match on two previous Lord's Test appearances in 1997 and 2001. By using the slope to perfection when bowling from the Pavilion end, he was well on his way to making it three awards in a row while decimating the English batting.

Left
Golden boots, golden touch - McGrath after dismissing Flintoff.

Below
Pietersen launches his Test career in attacking style.

reeling at 21 for five. All the euphoria at Lord's was now coloured green and gold as McGrath produced one of the greatest new ball spells the old ground has ever seen.

After being ten without loss at the interval, in the space of five overs England's batsmen were fighting for survival and credibility. Andrew Strauss edged McGrath to Shane Warne at slip, Michael Vaughan was bowled, as were Ian Bell and Andrew Flintoff. McGrath

Kevin Pietersen, on his Test debut, and Geraint Jones prevented the rout continuing before Brett Lee dismissed Jones and then forced Ashley Giles to tread on his wicket with the last ball of the day, leaving England on 92 for seven.

Hoggard went early next morning, so now Pietersen had license to attack. He did not waste the opportunity. He was receiving unlikely support from Harmison and had already hit Shane Warne for two sixes when he featured in what was to prove a turning point in the match. He swept Warne in the air towards the deep mid-wicket boundary. Martyn raced some 20 yards before diving full length to his left and backwards towards the rope to hold onto a two-handed catch. Another half hour of Pietersen in this mood and England could have enjoyed a useful lead. As it was, despite some entertaining hitting from

Below
Martyn deserves the adulation of his team mates after his sensational catch to dismiss Pietersen.

Harmison and Simon Jones, who added 33 for the last wicket, they had a deficit of 35.

The early loss of Langer, run out by a Pietersen direct hit, suggested that Australia could go cheaply again, but the lead was climbing to worrying proportions despite the wickets of Hayden, bowled by Flintoff, and Ponting. The Australian captain offered a simple catch to point off Hoggard that was accepted by substitute fielder James Hildreth. It was not the only time that Ponting would allow a substitute fielder his moment of glory in this series.

It was then that Pietersen featured in yet another potential turning point. He dropped a straightforward chance offered by Clarke in the covers off the luckless Simon Jones when the batsman had 21. It was the third catch that Pietersen had floored in the match, and by far his most costly miss. Clarke went on to make 91 in a partnership with Martyn that added 155 for the fourth wicket and took the game beyond England's reach. Had Pietersen not been out to a catch of such brilliance when he was, and had he not put down such a simple chance

Left
Elation for Flintoff and Pietersen as Langer is run out.

Below
Quality strokeplay from Clarke as Bell takes evasive action and wicket-keeper Jones looks on.

to reprieve Clarke when he did, England's target might have been manageable.

As it was, the lead was 290 when Clarke was eventually bowled by Hoggard. It had not increased when Martyn was lbw to Harmison. Gilchrist fell to Flintoff once

Right
Harmison applauds the run out of Lee as Katich looks aghast from the safety of the other end.

again, Warne was caught by Giles off Harmison and Australia closed the second day on 279 for seven. Lee was run out by Giles within four overs of the resumption next morning so with Australia at 289 for eight, England still had thoughts of an improbable victory with the pitch still good and so much time still available in the match.

They reckoned without the contribution of Simon Katich, who made 67 while supported by first Jason Gillespie and then McGrath. The last two wickets put on 95 runs that made the result a formality. England's cause was not helped when Geraint Jones put down two chances and Flintoff one off Simon Jones, who ended the innings by showing how it should be done when he caught Katich at third man off Harmison. England needed 420 to win.

With an opening partnership of 80 between Trescothick and Strauss, even that target did not seem impossible. However, the loss of five wickets for 39 in 13 overs before the close sealed England's fate. Well as the openers had batted, there was a feeling of impending

doom should either of them get out. Strauss was the first to do just that when, having battled his way to 37, he fended off a Lee thunderbolt in the direction of short mid-wicket. The ball went high enough for Lee to change direction in his follow-through, race to the on side of the pitch and throw himself forward to hold a two-handed catch just above the turf.

Trescothick was living dangerously against Warne, who was getting prodigious turn but no change out of umpire Aleem Dar despite the theatricality of his appeals, some of which, it must be said, looked totally vindicated by television replays. Eventually Warne got his man, caught by Hayden at slip, before Bell was lbw to the great leg-spinner.

When Vaughan was worryingly bowled again, this time by Lee, and Flintoff fell to Warne, the outcome was horribly evident to English eyes. Pietersen was still there on 42 with Geraint Jones on six when the third day came to a close with England 156 for five. All the euphoria of that first morning was long forgotten, for on a largely blameless pitch, 35 wickets had fallen in three days. There had been doubts about whether the English bowlers would be able to bowl out Australia twice to win a Test in this series. They had done their bit, but the batsmen had displayed all too familiar failings to leave England in a hopeless position at the end of the day.

All was not quite lost at the start of the fourth day, for the weather was doing its best to help the home cause. Heavy rain was falling and, with more forecast for the

Left
Lee takes a spectacular return catch to dismiss Strauss.

Right
England's dejected captain returns to the pavilion after being bowled by Lee.

Below
The weather was trying its best for England, but it was not enough to stave off defeat.

Far Right
First blood drawn - Australia in a huddle after going 1-0 up.

Monday, there were slim hopes that England might wriggle free. However, Harry Houdini did not appear among the batsmen still battling for survival. When play could finally get under way at 3.45 Jones went early, putting a weak pull against McGrath straight into mid-on's hands. It did not go down well when more rain was in the air. Giles steered his second ball to gully and McGrath was rampant again.

Hoggard's usually lumbering gait was slower than usual as he made his way to the middle, before another shower lifted hopes of redemption. They were short lived. On the resumption, McGrath delivered a succession of short balls before bringing a full-length delivery back down the slope to have Hoggard lbw. Harmison was also lbw, this time to Warne leaving England on 167 for nine. Pietersen had time to reach his second fifty of the match and continue unbowed and undefeated on 64, as Simon Jones went to McGrath. England 180 all out. Australia the winners by 239 runs.

It appeared to be a massive margin, and in reality it was. However, scorecards can sometimes mask the truth or magnify the difference between sides. Had Martyn not held that catch in the first innings and had Pietersen not dropped his in the second, it would have been very much closer. Without the huge target, England could have retained some hope while Australia could not have set relentlessly attacking fields. In fact, the outcome might have been entirely different.

It would be entirely different before the end of the next match, and the result at Lord's in no way warranted the chorus of "here we go again" that, understandably, could be heard from London to Sydney.

1 & 2 BEDROOM APARTMENTS
EDGBASTON ROAD, EDGBASTON
TELEPHONE 0121 504 0288
www.redrow.co.uk
ERPETUAL ISAs
ebookers.com
Red Stripe
WOLF BLASS W

Chapter Two
Edgbaston

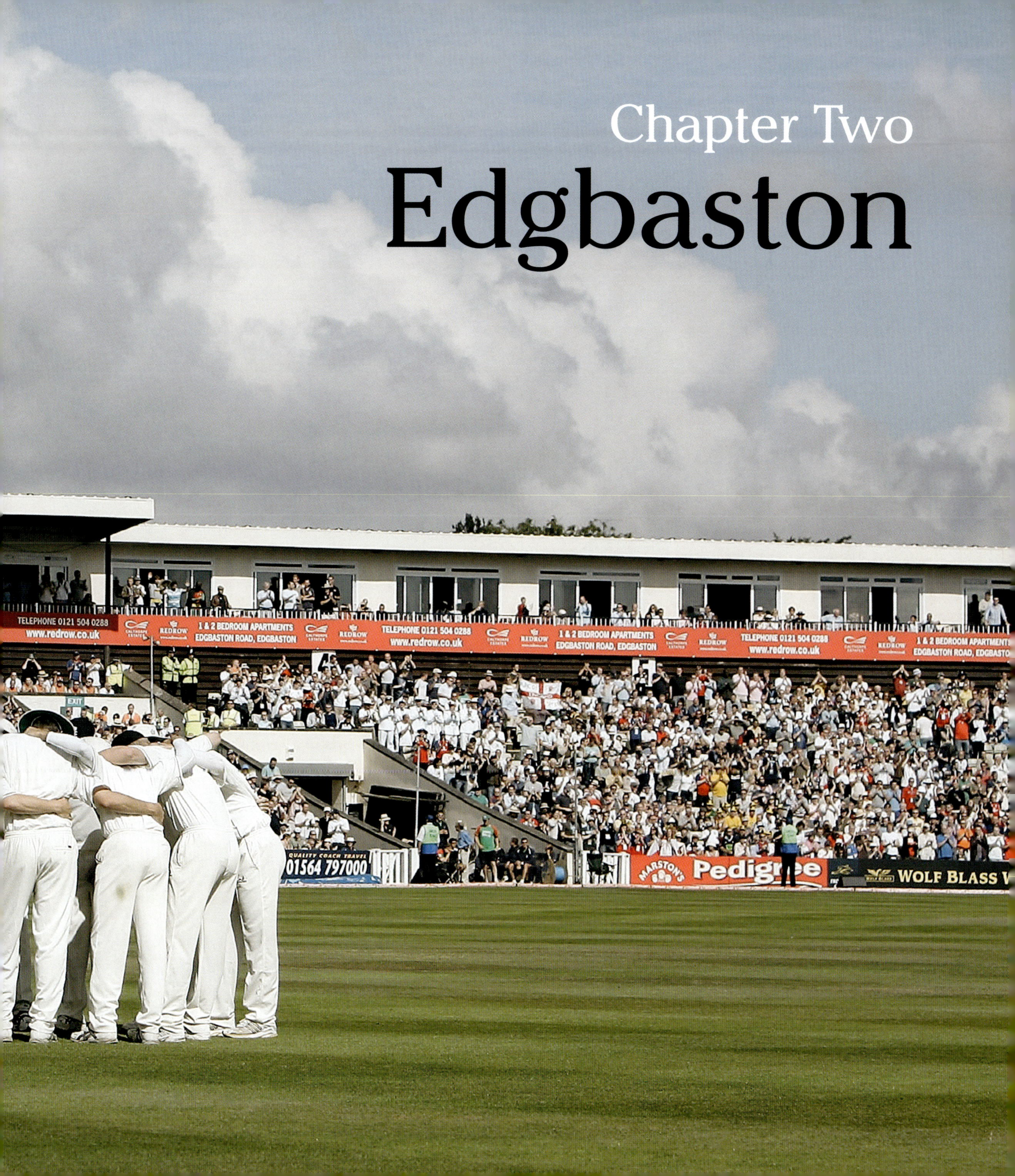

THERE are times when it is only with hindsight that the true significance of a chance occurrence becomes evident. At Edgbaston on the morning of August 4th, something happened that shone out like a beacon on a stormy night. The Australian hero of Lord's, Glenn McGrath, was taking part in a game of touch rugby as a means of warming up for the forthcoming second Test. A cricket ball had been left on the ground after fielding practice and as McGrath came down from catching a pass, he landed on the stray ball and turned his ankle.

As he was carried from the field on a golf buggy, England's hopes flickered. When the news that he was unable to take part in the match was confirmed, those hopes ignited. It was generally regarded as being England's last chance – not only to get back into contention for the Ashes but also to keep cricket in the forefront of public attention after the defeat at Lord's and before the impending start of a new football season. That thought simply added to the excitement of the last session; with such a prize or such a penalty at stake, the tension of the final moments was almost indescribable.

To add to England's joy, Australian captain Ricky Ponting won the toss and for reasons never satisfactorily explained, decided to invite England to take first use of a wicket that appeared full of runs. Had McGrath been fit, there was an argument to back up Ponting's decision on the basis that he might exploit demons in England's batting psyche lurking from Lord's. But McGrath was not fit. Had Ponting not had the world's best exponent of bowling on a fifth day pitch in his ranks, he might have thought of putting England in. But he did have Shane Warne at his disposal. All that is known is that he had plenty of time to rue his decision.

Not that he had much time to think such thoughts when he took the field, because England had decided on a policy of abandoning introspection and taking the attack to the Australians. In turn, Australia refused to accept that their long superiority was being seriously challenged until the last ball was bowled and they were still three runs away from victory.

Left
Twist of fate - McGrath leaves the field after treading on a stray ball while warming up for the Edgbaston Test.

Above
Gilchrist looks on helplessly as Trescothick launches England with a flourish.

The new approach from England was evident from the outset being bowled out in 80 overs, they reached the impressive total of 407. Marcus Trescothick's 90 at the top of the innings was important in setting the tone. He and Andrew Strauss put on 112 for the first wicket at four an over, with the pair taking particular delight in depositing Warne into the outfield or beyond for priceless runs.

Strauss was out shortly before the lunch interval, attempting to cut a ball that was too close to him and which turned appreciably. Trescothick continued to attack and looked set for a hundred, at least, before

hanging his bat out to edge Michael Kasprowicz to the 'keeper. Ian Bell went the same way to a rather better ball, and Michael Vaughan top-edged a hook against Jason Gillespie to fine leg where Brett Lee took a good catch. England 187 for 4 after 37 overs of play.

From the moment Kevin Pietersen and Andrew Flintoff had been named in the same team, there had been expectations of explosive batting in England's middle order. For a variety of reasons, the fireworks had not ignited, until now. Their partnership of 103 inside 18 overs not only provided great entertainment but also shredded the Australian attack and fielders, who suddenly started to make mistakes not usually associated with this side.

Far Left
The top-edged hook off Gillespie that brought about Vaughan's downfall.

Left
Flintoff hooks with power and balance during his dazzling stand with Pietersen.

Right
Australian frustration mounts as Harmison joins England's boundary bonanza.

Flintoff began without conviction, especially against Warne, but a couple of thumping boundaries restored his self-belief. Pietersen has never suffered a shortage in that area and the pair went blow for blow, shot for shot and run for run. When Lee bowled a fierce spell against Flintoff, he was counter-attacked with three hooks of a ferocity to stir the soul. Comparisons with Ian Botham have never been fair on Flintoff, but one still photograph of a Flintoff six revealed that he got as much sight of the ball as did Botham when hooking Dennis Lillee in 1981. None.

It was Jason Gillespie who ended the entertainment by getting Flintoff to edge behind and so claim his 250th Test wicket. The torment for Australia did not end there, although Geraint Jones got a ball that lifted and went cheaply so England were 293 for six. Bearing in mind the fact that none of the final four batsmen had got a run in England's second innings at Lord's, Ponting might have held hopes of justifying his decision at the toss by taking the last wickets cheaply again.

Ashley Giles had other ideas, contributing 49 with Pietersen before falling lbw to Warne. Pietersen added one more six to his tally before being caught on the boundary to end an innings containing some extraordinary and exciting strokes, but Matthew Hoggard, Stephen Harmison and Simon Jones had some fun of their own, making 59 for the last three wickets. 407 runs in 80 overs. Conditions did not allow Australia to bat that day, but there were few spectators who could have any grounds for complaint that the day was ten overs short of the quota.

Day two belonged to England as well. Matthew Hayden went early to Hoggard, and just as Ponting looked to be getting going, he top-edged a sweep against Giles to Vaughan at short fine leg. The England captain featured again just before lunch when, off balance, he swooped, pivoted and hit the stumps at the bowler's end from side on with Damien Martyn no more than an inch out. It was an astonishing piece of fielding after a moment's hesitation from Martyn.

After the interval Giles struck again, this time to remove Michael Clarke with a quicker ball. After Flintoff had claimed Simon Katich, Simon Jones began to make the ball reverse swing around corners. He snared the adhesive Justin Langer and the dangerous Lee. Giles accounted for Warne thanks to an ungainly heave from a batsman who had two first-class hundreds for Hampshire earlier in the season, and Flintoff ripped out Gillespie and Kasprowicz to leave Gilchrist stranded and Australia with a deficit of 99.

Above
He who hesitates is lost – Martyn narrowly run out by a brilliant throw from Vaughan.

Left
Euphoric reaction from England's captain follows Martyn's dismissal.

There was still time for something more out of the ordinary in the final overs of the day when England batted again. Trescothick and Strauss paid scant heed to what is usually referred to as “a tricky little session” before Warne conjured something out of nothing. If Mike Gatting had been bowled at Old Trafford in 1993 by Warne’s “ball of the century”, Strauss went to Warne’s ball of the 21st century. As unlikely as it might seem, it turned out of the footmarks a distance of three feet from pitching to hitting the stumps. Strauss was left looking befuddled and aggrieved to have been the victim of such an outrageous piece of bowling.

England’s batting early on the third day disappointed both them and their legions of supporters who had given full-throated support throughout. Trescothick went quickly, so too did Vaughan and nightwatchman Hoggard. Bell and Pietersen promised to go on but, having reached the twenties, both fell to Warne and at 75 for six, England faced real problems. A lead of 174 with four wickets standing between Australia and a two-nil lead in the Ashes. One of those wickets, however, belonged to Flintoff and he was not going to surrender it cheaply.

His efforts were even more admirable in light of the perilous situation that faced his team and the fact that he suffered a freak injury just before lunch. In playing a ball into the off side, the big man tweaked something in his shoulder and was seriously incapacitated. To face the likes of Warne and Lee fully fit is one thing; to face them virtually one-handed is quite another.

Flintoff appeared to be moving more freely after lunch but he lost another partner when Geraint Jones got a ball from Lee in the first over after the interval that lifted

Right
Flintoff’s injured shoulder receives attention from England physio Kirk Russell.

fiercely and he could do no more than fend it off into the waiting hands of Ponting at slip. Warne took his wicket tally to five in the innings by dismissing Giles and Harmison in successive balls to leave England on 131 for nine.

With only Simon Jones to bat, it was the signal for Flintoff to launch a counter-attack. It was a foretaste of what Pietersen was to do after lunch on the fifth day at the Oval. Flintoff began by hitting two towering sixes as he took 20 off a single over from Kasprowicz. Then he turned his big guns on Lee. The result was a six straight driven out of the arena, four and another six, despite the fact that the nine fielders were all posted on the boundary. To have any chance of catching the ball they would have needed to buy seats in row E at least.

Simon Jones was playing his part as well, facing 23 balls as he kept Flintoff company for nearly three quarters of an hour during which time he added 12 runs – all boundaries – of his own and helped to dent Australian morale. When Warne ended Flintoff's innings to pick up his tenth wicket in the match, England had a lead of 281. With so much time left in the game it was not an impossible target, provided the Australians began well.

Left
Flintoff makes light of his injury with a majestic straight six under the approving gaze of Gilchrist.

Above
Giles and England cock-a-hoop after Gilchrist holes out at mid-on.

The balance of the game then fluctuated wildly as Australia seemed to gain the initiative before England took it back once more. When Hayden and Martyn were together, it looked as if England had fallen some way short of setting a competitive target. But when Simon Jones came back from being hit for two fours to have Hayden caught behind, and Hoggard returned to the attack to get Martyn caught off his first ball, things were definitely going England's way.

It was Giles who confirmed that trend by taking the next two wickets. Katich edged the left-arm spinner to slip before Gilchrist was lured into an indiscretion that resulted in a catch at mid-on. Perhaps Australian thinking was still scrambled, because Gillespie was sent in as nightwatchman. He lasted two balls before getting his pad in the way of a straight one from Flintoff.

Thanks to Langer and Hayden, they did indeed get the required start. Almost four an over for the first 12 before that man Flintoff struck again. He had started his spell on a hat-trick and, while he did not manage to complete that, he did bowl what was perhaps the over of the summer. All Langer could do with the second ball was to edge it onto his stumps. Ponting somehow negotiated three balls but edged the fourth to Geraint Jones and England were on their way.

England claimed the extra half hour in search of the win that evening. The response of Warne, who had joined Clarke, was to hit Giles for two sixes. As the last over of the day began, Australia had reached 175 for seven. Clarke was batting fluently, while Warne was known to be

a dangerous proposition with a bat in his hand. England were still favourites, but Australia were moving closer.

After his success at Lord's, Harmison had gone wicketless at Edgbaston. Nevertheless, the next two wickets he took would prove priceless in the context of the series. With the fourth ball of this final over of the day, Harmison produced a magnificent slower yorker to bowl Clarke and swing affairs perhaps decisively towards England. 107 runs still needed by Australia and only two wickets required by England. All the talk overnight was of it taking only two balls on the morrow to square the series.

Above
Pumped up – Harmison rouses England with the crucial scalp of Clarke.

Right
Foot fault – the bizarre end to Warne's tenacious innings of 42 that had rekindled Australian hopes.

Below
As Warne turns in disbelief, Flintoff launches the England celebrations.

It took rather longer than that as Warne added 45 for the ninth wicket with Lee. The pair took few chances and offered even less. Both batsmen grew in confidence, the English faces began to betray signs of slight anxiety. The crowd too grew less vociferous as the batsmen showed more belief than the bowlers.

That all changed when Flintoff bowled at Warne's pads and the batsman went back to flick it off his legs. He missed and his foot dislodged the bails. 62 more needed and the last pair at the wicket.

Lee and Kasprowicz began chipping away at the target. Runs came from deflections off the

quicks, from leg byes as the attack grew tense and wayward, while Giles went for 13 in one over. That slight anxiety became real concern. Even the Barmy Army went quiet as each ball was bowled.

When the target had been reduced to a mere 15, and the odds were starting to favour an Australian win, Flintoff bowled wide of off stump, Kasprowicz went after it and the ball flew down towards third man. Simon Jones took a moment to pick up the flight, which is never easy in that position, and bravely dived forward to take the catch that would have won the match. He could not hold on to it. Was that going to be the last chance?

More runs came. The tension increased. Strong men could not bear to watch. The more the bowlers strained for that magic ball, the more elusive it became. From 62 being needed when the last pair came

Below
Relief of a nation – ecstasy for England as Kasprowicz's dismissal secures a two-run win.

Right
Sporting gesture: as England celebrate, Flintoff has a consoling word for Lee.

Below Right
Brothers in arms – Harmison and Flintoff acknowledge the Edgbaston applause.

together, there were now only three. Kasprowicz faced Harmison who knew that one wayward ball would end the match, and in all probablity the revival that English cricket had been enjoying.

Harmison got away with two balls, but the third was dangerously towards the leg side. Kasprowicz fended it off; the ball could have flown anywhere. In fact, it looped over the batsman's head far enough for the not infallible Geraint Jones to tumble to his left and hang on. Umpire Billy Bowden's crooked index finger was raised

and it was probably as much relief as joy that fuelled the prolonged, ecstatic celebrations among the English team and supporters. The two-run margin of victory was the second narrowest in Test history.

Chapter Three

Old Trafford

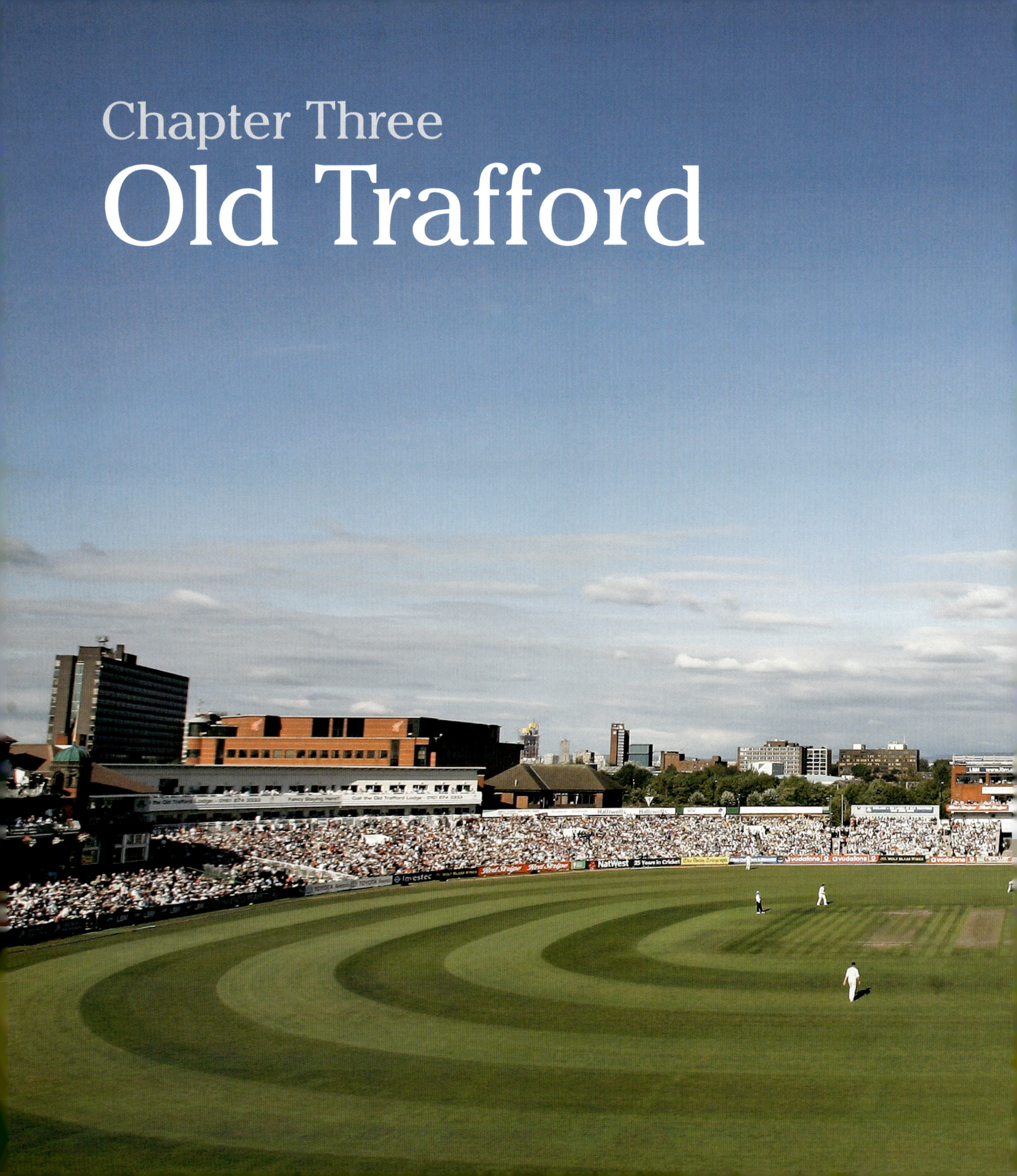

npower
Ashes Test Series
betfair.com
vodafone
TOYOTA
THWAITES BEERS

IF Ricky Ponting had been misled by the bizarre weather conditions before the Edgbaston Test, he would have had no doubt about what to do if he won the toss at Old Trafford. Unfortunately for him and for Australia, his luck in that department had run out for the series. Michael Vaughan had no hesitation in batting on what turned out to be a golden day for the England captain.

Although Australia were relieved to welcome back Glenn McGrath following his freak injury at Edgbaston, batting first would have given him more recovery time. In the event he was bowling the first over of the match, with

Brett Lee also included despite being hospitalised with a knee infection just two days earlier. The two shared the new ball, and with better support from their fielders might have put Australia in control. Australia also suffered a setback when Michael Clarke left the field after just two overs with a lower back problem. He was not to field again in the match.

The usually reliable Adam Gilchrist was the culprit in the first session, missing Marcus Trescothick on 13 and Vaughan on 41, both off McGrath and both with expensive results. After the Somerset left-hander had been missed in the fifth over as Gilchrist snatched one

Left
Pain in the neck – Strauss is hit by an express delivery from Lee on the first morning at Old Trafford.

handed at an edged dive, Andrew Strauss went early for six. It was a deserved wicket for a fired-up Brett Lee, who produced a series of bouncers travelling at between 96 and 97mph., one of which hit Strauss on the neck as he tried to hook. In Lee's next over, Strauss played too early at a slower delivery which plucked out his off stump. It was Lee's 150th Test wicket.

Enter Vaughan, hitherto short of runs, but with a spring in his step on a ground where he had succeeded for England before and in the city in which he was born. He began patiently, but accelerated along with Trescothick when Jason Gillespie was brought into the attack, again with expensive results. He went for 33 runs in his first six overs, and was driven through the covers by

Above
Gilchrist looks in anguish towards third man, after failing to cling on to an edge from Vaughan.

Right
Change of pace – Lee celebrates removing Strauss's off stump with a slower ball.

Vaughan in a manner just hinting at disdain. But in the 29th over, McGrath's tenth, came one of those moments, or in fact two, of critical importance. Vaughan, on 41, was missed by Gilchrist, diving to his right and parrying the ball to the third man boundary. The next delivery, a no ball, knocked out Vaughan's off stump. He was to score another 125 runs before being dismissed.

Vaughan's partnership with Trescothick had reached 137, a second wicket record against Australia on this ground, when a piece of remarkable history was made. Shane Warne, who wasn't brought on by Ponting until the 34th over, induced an attempted sweep from Trescothick that flew off the back of his bat for Gilchrist to cling on to the ball at the second attempt. On the ground where he burst so sensationally on to the Ashes scene with the "ball of the century" 12 years earlier, Warne had taken his

Left
McGrath's face says it all after Vaughan is bowled by a no ball.

Below
History in the making as Gilchrist catches Trescothick to give Warne his 600th Test wicket.

Right
Contrasting emotions as Gillespie is punished again by a rampant Vaughan.

600th Test wicket, becoming the first bowler ever to do so. He held up the ball, took off his sunhat and waved to acknowledge the heartfelt and extended roar of applause from the Manchester crowd.

Vaughan now went from strength to strength, tolling the bell for Gillespie, whom he hit for ten fours and a pulled six over midwicket. At last the England captain was showing the form that had so delighted cricket lovers earlier in the decade, and had threatened Australia in the previous series down under. He was missed again on 141, by Matthew Hayden at slip off Warne, and Ian Bell, another batsman in need of runs, profited on 18 when McGrath put down a straightforward return catch. Vaughan's wonderful display of elegance finally ended when he pulled loosely at the part-timer Simon Katich for McGrath to hold on at deep mid-wicket. It was a soft dismissal and Vaughan could scarcely believe it. He had faced 216 balls and hit a six and 21 fours.

Above
Flintoff cuts during his 46 that helped to push England's first innings total beyond 400.

Having at one stage been 290 for two, England would have been disappointed to end the day on 341 for five. Australia took the new ball and Kevin Pietersen ill-advisedly pulled Lee straight to the substitute fielder, Brad Hodge, at deep midwicket. And the Nightwatchman Matthew Hoggard fell to the last ball of the day, a searing Lee yorker. But the ship was steadied the following morning by Andrew Flintoff and Geraint Jones, who again shared a profitable partnership, this time of 87, after Bell had gone early for 59, gloving an attempted hook off Lee. Although each fell narrowly short of a half- century, Flintoff and Jones ensured a respectable total of 444.

Hayden and Justin Langer now joined forces to post their first half-century partnership of the series, and while they were together first innings parity looked distinctly possible on a good wicket. But England's bowlers, in much the same way as at Edgbaston, simply refused to be deflected from their strategy and purpose. To the increasing delight of the Old Trafford crowd, Australia's

Above
Dream catch – Bell is mobbed by team mates after a reflex effort at short leg to send back Langer.

top order was steadily chiselled out without any batsman becoming established.

Langer departed first to a magnificent, one-handed reflex catch by Bell at short leg in Ashley Giles' first over. Bell then had not one hand, but both, in the important dismissal of Australia's captain to the first ball after lunch, which Simon Jones got to lift awkwardly and loop off the edge of Ponting's bat, straight to gully. 73-2 became 86-3 when Hayden was given out lbw to Giles, who now produced one of the best balls of his life, spinning from the leg side to hit the top of Damien Martyn's off stump. By then Katich had gone as well, suckered by Flintoff,

who bowled a succession of leavable deliveries outside off stump. Straight after a drinks break, he swung one back in; Katich left it and was castled.

A taxi was now summoned for Clarke, who was resting his back at the team hotel, but while he was on his way to the ground England were suddenly afflicted by the Australian malaise of the previous day. Gilchrist was twice dropped off Flintoff, first by Bell at backward point and then by Pietersen at cover. Neither chance was easy or particularly expensive. With Gilchrist and Warne

Above
Fred'll fix it – more joy for England after Flintoff dismisses Katich.

threatening a genuine rally Jones struck, yet again, with the first ball of a new spell. Gilchrist, cramped for room as he tried to cut, was caught behind and Clarke, in obvious discomfort and batting with a runner, drove a slower ball to mid off. At 201 for seven, Australia were in danger of being forced to follow on for the first time since 1988.

It was Warne the batsman, having ended day two unbeaten on 45, who ensured that they avoided such indignity, although the England coach, Duncan Fletcher, later gave a strong hint that they would have batted anyway. After rain had delayed the start on day three until four o'clock, just two short sessions were possible, of

Right
Not again – Gilchrist's body language says it all after edging one Jones to another.

eight and six overs. In the first, Warne and Gillespie took Australia past the follow-on target, but Warne, on 55, won the first of two reprieves from Geraint Jones, who missed a stumping off Giles. In the second session he grassed a straightforward nick off Flintoff in bright, possibly dazzling, sunshine. It was a bizarre end to a wretched day, truncated to a degree that was to have critical implications for England's pursuit of victory.

Warne's hopes of a maiden Test century were dashed just ten runs short of the target. After adding 12 runs on

Below
Misery for the Manchester spectators as rain reduces play on day three to just 14 overs.

Above
Warne swings Giles away during his first innings 90 for Australia.

the fourth morning he became another victim of Simon Jones' ability to strike early in a spell, hitting his second delivery straight to Giles at deep square leg. Jones then cleaned up, first luring Lee into a drive at an away swinger and finding the edge for Trescothick to take the catch, diving to his left at slip. Gillespie's 111-ball vigil, which had started two days earlier, came to an end as he was lbw to a ball of full length that swung in from outside his leg stump. Australia had surrendered a first innings lead of 142 and Jones had finished with career-best figures of six for 53.

Left
That'll be five then! Jones celebrates graphically as Lee heads for the pavilion.

It said much for the collective character of the England team that invariably during this wonderfully engrossing series, someone stood up to be counted when it was required. Going into this game Strauss, Vaughan and Bell were all in need of runs, so it reflected the overall tone, after two had succeeded in the first innings, that the third should do so in the second. By the end of the fourth day Warne was perhaps ruing his remarks before the match about how much he looked forward to bowling at Strauss, his new "Daryl" (after Daryl Cullinan, the South African batsman whom Warne had so regularly bewitched in earlier years).

Again, the Australians let themselves down in the field, uncannily resembling the butter-fingered England

team of four years earlier. After Strauss had again been hit by Lee, who this time drew blood from a cut ear, he edged him between Warne and Ponting in the slips. It was catchable for either, but they simply stood and watched the ball fly to the third man boundary. Trescothick, meanwhile, was giving the innings perfect impetus at the outset, with a succession of booming drives and cuts which took him to 41 off 56 balls before he played at one from McGrath which span back to hit his off stump.

Vaughan could not continue the eye-catching mastery of his first innings, top-edging a pull to fine leg where Hodge, still subbing for Clarke, took a fine catch on his knees close to the boundary. But Bell now joined Strauss to begin the partnership that was to form the backbone of the innings. Each batsman moved along steadily, but as the England lead extended beyond 300, they expressed themselves more freely. Strauss, his Warne demons conquered for the present at least, moved into the

Below
Clean sweep – Trescothick swings low during his second innings 41.

Right
A characteristic pull from Strauss during the Middlesex opener's maiden Ashes century.

Left
Done it! Strauss is a picture of delight after composing his first hundred against England's oldest enemy.

nineties with a trademark pull for six before executing another to complete his first hundred against Australia. In keeping with the spirit of the series, Warne gave the overjoyed Strauss a shake of the hand and a pat on the back.

With the pressure off England and Australia feeling all the heat, Strauss departed with a pull to Martyn at deep square leg, but Bell was now showing signs of real class, driving McGrath through the covers for four and over long off for six, not an occurrence often associated with the great New South Welshman. Gilchrist compounded Australia's woes by twice failing to stump Bell as he moved down the track to Warne, and Australia were looking as ragged in the field as they had done for many years. Bell eventually fell for 65 as McGrath picked up a flurry of irrelevant wickets with the declaration imminent. Geraint Jones twice hoisted him over the midwicket boundary in a 12-ball 27 before Vaughan called time. Although Langer and Hayden

Above
A touch of class – Ian Bell during his second half century of the match at Old Trafford.

Right
Flintoff salutes the crowd after dismissing Katich for the second time in the match.

survived to the close it had been Australia's worst day of the series so far, and the victory target of 423 looked mountainous.

With wonderful symmetry on the final day, Ponting played an innings that was no less vital to Australia than Vaughan's had been for England on day one. He arrived at the crease in the second over after Hoggard's first ball, a perfect outswinger, had kissed Langer's edge on its way through to Jones. Flintoff bowled Hayden behind his legs, and when Martyn was given out lbw to Harmison, Australia were teetering at 129 for three. Despite Ponting's continued stoic resistance the situation worsened when Giles brilliantly caught Katich above his head at third slip off the Herculean Flintoff. A failure for Gilchrist, slashing Flintoff to Bell in the gully, and Australia were 182 for five.

Left
Joy for Hoggard as Langer edges his first ball of the day to Geraint Jones.

Right
He ain't heavy – a fireman's lift for Hoggard after Flintoff snares Warne.

Clarke, moving more easily than in the first innings, now made provided Ponting with the partner he desperately needed. Not allowing the situation to cramp his style, Clarke made an eye-catching 39 and had added 81 with Ponting when he fell to Jones' reverse swing, losing his off stump. When Hoggard trapped Gillespie lbw, England had 29 overs to take three wickets. But no one enjoys spiking English guns more than Warne, who batted with such panache, for the second time in the match, that it briefly seemed conceivable that Australia might win it. Warne had a slice of luck when he clipped a Jones full toss to midwicket, only for Pietersen to miss his fifth chance of the series.

Crucially, Ponting and Warne stayed together for 22 overs, and it took an unimaginable piece of drama to part them. Warne, on 34, edged Flintoff to Strauss who could only parry the ball at second slip. With commendable speed of reaction, Geraint Jones dived away behind him to hold the rebound and Warne had to go. For anyone fortunate enough to be at Old Trafford (20,000 had been turned away that morning), the atmosphere was now feverish in its intensity.

With his job more than 90 per cent done, Ponting now fell victim, in part, to his own desire to keep Lee off strike. With just 25 balls left in the match, he got into a tangle attempting

Left
Ponting takes a sharp single during his match-saving knock of 156 on day five.

Right
The last equation – the scoreboard says it all as the game approaches its nerve-jangling finish.

Far Right
Grins of relief from Lee and McGrath after Australia hold out to keep the series at one all.

to pull Harmison, succeeding only in gloving a catch to Geraint Jones. England were down to Australia's last-wicket pair of Lee and McGrath. Edgbaston, eat your heart out! As the two defended dourly, Simon Jones had to leave the field with cramp. The last over, bowled by Harmison, was enough to shred nerves of steel. McGrath took a single off the third ball, and Lee did not need to play the next two. The final delivery was pushed down to fine leg and Lee lifted his arms in triumph before leaving the arena with McGrath in celebration. Whoever said that draws were dull?

Chapter Four

Trent Bridge

EVENING POST
Investec
INVESCO PERPETUAL

AFTER the back-to-back second and third Tests, there was time for the players and spectators to draw breath, re-group and prepare for the next chapter of the epic saga that was the Ashes 2005. The question that everyone was asking centred on whether elegant Trent Bridge could match the drama of Edgbaston or the tension of Old Trafford. After another pulsating four days of cricket, the answer was that it most definitely could.

Michael Vaughan won an all-important toss and had no hesitation in batting on a pitch that appeared to be overflowing with runs. Furthermore, the Australians were once again without Glenn McGrath, this time because of an elbow injury, while they had decided before the match that time had run out for Jason Gillespie. He had not hit rhythm at any time during the tour and was now being targeted by the England batsmen. Shaun Tait, fresh from an outstanding season in domestic cricket back home, made his Test debut and with Michael Kasprowicz being recalled in place of the injured McGrath, the attack appeared a little thin.

It seemed positively threadbare as the openers rattled along to 105 at nearly five an over before the first wicket fell. Once again, Ricky Ponting had been forced to bowl Shane Warne on the first morning and once again the leg-spinner accounted for Andrew Strauss. He went to sweep but deflected the ball onto his boot before it looped up to Matthew Hayden at slip and the third umpire found in the bowler's favour. It was a bizarre way to get out, but at that stage in proceedings Australia were not going to complain.

Marcus Trescothick had hit Warne for an imperious straight six on his introduction to the attack, but his was the next wicket to fall. It was some time after the lunch interval, because heavy

Left
Shaun Tait at the point of delivery on his Test debut at Trent Bridge.

Above
England's opening partnership of 105 ends as Strauss is caught by Hayden off Warne.

showers restricted the afternoon session to just three overs and one ball. The stoppage meant that the Australian bowlers could regroup and rethink their attack. Trescothick had enjoyed one let-off when he dragged a ball from Brett Lee onto his stumps. The Australians celebrated, the batsman made off towards the pavilion, only to be aware of a reprieve as umpire Steve Bucknor signalled one of 22 no balls bowled in the day.

The end for Trescothick, though, was not long in coming. Tait had been registering in the mid-nineties on the speedgun and was better in his second spell than when understandably nervous in his first. He bowled

Left
Role reversal for Ponting as Australia's captain has his opposite number caught behind.

Trescothick and then saw Ian Bell edge a good, quick outswinger to Adam Gilchrist. Australia were clawing their way back – a process hastened when the England captain gave his wicket to his opposite number.

Vaughan and Kevin Pietersen had restored England's grip on the game as the shortened first day neared its conclusion. They had been careful about which balls to attack, but Vaughan looked set for another major innings following his efforts at Old Trafford. Ponting had exhausted his limited bowling options to the extent that he brought himself on in an effort to break the burgeoning partnership.

The batsmen were keen not to get out to his medium pace, but that can be a valuable weapon for an occasional bowler. To come through Lee and Tait unscathed and then nibble at a goodish ball from Ponting as Vaughan did to be caught behind is akin to completing a formula one grand prix only to collide with a shopping trolley when stopping off at Tesco's on the way home. No wonder Vaughan looked aghast while Ponting enjoyed one of his better moments in the field as England closed the first day on 229 for four.

The Flintoff-Pietersen partnership was destined to be short-lived on this occasion. In fact, it had only limped into the fifth over of the second day when Pietersen was caught behind off Lee. Flintoff was joined by the last of the recognised batsmen, Geraint Jones. Papua New Guinea, where Jones was born, does not have a record for producing outstanding Test wicket-keeper/batsmen, but Kent, where Jones plies his trade, does. The quality of his wicket-keeping has been a discussion point since he was first selected for England, and will no doubt continue to be so.

The facts are that in the 20 Tests he had played by the end of this Ashes series, he had taken 71 catches and made three stumpings. It is also generally reckoned that

Below
Gilchrist watches as Geraint Jones prepares to sweep another boundary during his first innings 85.

he has missed 15 chances in those matches while conceding 199 byes. They are not figures that compare favourably with county and national predecessors like Alan Knott and Godfrey Evans. The reason for his continued inclusion was his potential with the bat. He might have ended the series with his Test average still just below 30 but on this day at Trent Bridge, he entirely justified his place in the team.

In partnership with Flintoff, Jones added 177 for the sixth wicket. Flintoff was majestic in going to his first Ashes hundred, and displayed his growing maturity when facing Warne in the nineties. He forsook the rasping strokes that had propelled him towards three figures, and instead refused to be tempted by the balls pitching in the rough outside his leg stump. He waited and waited until the right ball came along and simply clipped it away to reach the personal milestone that meant so much to him.

He was out shortly after reaching his century, lbw to Tait, whom he had punished so mercilessly when the youngster took the new ball. Jones, who was batting well enough to get a hundred of his own, fell to Kasprowicz on 85 as an inside edge ballooned back down the pitch off his pad for the bowler to take an accomplished return catch, low down on the leg side. But England were not done yet. The tail, or lower order as they prefer to be known, withstood Warne well enough to reach 477, England's third consecutive first innings total above 400.

Left
Flintoff acknowledges a standing ovation after reaching a crucial hundred.

Above
England fielders converge on Hoggard after the Yorkshireman dismissed Hayden for seven.

Compared to England's uninhibited attacking batting, Australia's reply was somewhat staid. Justin Langer and Matthew Hayden had scored only 20 in the tenth over when Hayden was lbw to Matthew Hoggard. The Yorkshireman found the swinging conditions very much to his liking, keeping the umpires on their toes as the Australian batsmen shuffled across the crease. It was Hoggard's turn for a place in the sun.

Ponting was pinned to the crease by Simon Jones before Hoggard struck again for a similar decision against Damien Martyn, who could be considered hard done by after replays revealed a certain amount of bat on the ball before pad. Hoggard's third wicket came when Langer gloved a lifting ball to Bell at short leg, in the over after he had been struck a ringing blow on the helmet by Flintoff. Harmison was brought back for the last over of the day to bowl to Michael Clarke who looked capable of thwarting England's plans. However, just as at Edgbaston, Harmison was too good for him. There was no doubt about the fourth lbw of the day which ended with Australia struggling on 99 for five.

Simon Katich and especially Gilchrist went on the offensive next morning. Gilchrist had never been in a position during the series to impose himself on the bowling as he can. The situation was not much different this time, but he had obviously decided that the careful, considered approach had not worked, so a bit of dash

and bravado might not be out of place. He lost Katich to a catch by Strauss at slip off Simon Jones who, next ball, turned Warne this way and that before he popped up a catch to short leg.

If the catch that Strauss held to send back Katich was reasonably straightforward, the one with which he dismissed Gilchrist was out of the very top drawer. Flintoff was the bowler and Gilchrist went hard at it. It was destined to bisect the slips when Strauss took off to his left to hold a quite stunning catch inches off the ground and while he was horizontal at full stretch. As the soon to be retired Richie Benaud might have said, "catches don't come any better than that!"

Lee played some blistering shots to reach 47 from 44 balls, but just as Simon Jones had removed Kasprowicz, so he accounted for Lee to end a last wicket partnership of 43 and to secure his five-wicket haul. Australia all out for 218 and asked to follow on. It must have been a sweet moment for Vaughan to knock on the Australian dressing room door and tell them that they could bat again. Nobody had been able to do that since 1988, or 191 Tests ago.

Above
Strauss comes to earth to complete the catch of the series to dismiss Gilchrist.

Above
Simon Jones is forced to watch from the pavilion after limping from the field with an ankle injury.

Below
The run out that preceded Ponting's verbal outburst after Australia were forced to follow on.

Right
Substitute fielder Gary Pratt is mobbed by team mates after achieving the run out with a direct hit.

The moment would have lost some of its sweetness when, after taking the new ball, Simon Jones limped from the field with an ankle injury. The pitch looked rather flat as Hayden and Langer managed to complete a fifty partnership for only the second time in the series, but no sooner had they done so than Flintoff picked up Hayden with a catch to Giles in the gully. Flintoff should also have had Langer, but Strauss floored a comparatively straightforward chance and it was not until Giles had his first bowl of the match that Langer was out, caught at short leg by Bell.

That brought Martyn in to join his captain, who was going easily with some fine strokeplay. It took one of the talking points of the series to remove him. Martyn called Ponting for a single, but substitute fielder Gary Pratt swooped in the covers and ran out Ponting with a direct hit. Ponting was unhappy that England bowlers frequently went off to recuperate at the end of a spell. This time, however, Pratt was on the field while Simon Jones was in hospital having an x-ray on his injured ankle. Not only that, but Pratt is a specialist fielder of renown, adding to Ponting's displeasure that he made clear to all and sundry right up until he walked up the pavilion steps, still mouthing at the England dressing room.

Martyn followed six runs later, caught behind off Flintoff, but Clarke and Katich once again steadied the badly-listing Australian vessel. Clarke was aided by a bad stumping miss by Jones off Giles, but at 222 for four at the early close for bad light, the pair had added 61 runs and halted England's charge, for the time being at least.

England wanted wickets before the arrears of 259 were wiped off, but despite what must have been a close call against Clarke by Hoggard, no wicket came. This was where Vaughan earned his corn as captain. He wanted wickets, but he knew that he could not afford to chase too large a total in the fourth innings with a certain blond leg-spinner in the opposing ranks. Clarke and Katich had put on exactly 100 when England at last broke through, Hoggard moving one away from Clarke to find the edge and thence wicket-keeper Jones' gloves.

Only one wicket in the morning session was not what England wanted, but they had to settle for that and show patience. It was rewarded after the interval when Gilchrist, who had hit consecutive fours off Flintoff just before lunch, was out lbw to Hoggard. Warne went one better than

Left
Hoggard celebrates a crucial breakthrough after having Clarke caught behind for 56.

Gilchrist with three fours off Flintoff in an over, but he lost Katich to yet another lbw decision. Harmison appeared to have pitched some way outside leg stump and too short for the ball to hit the stumps. Nevertheless, a clearly furious Katich was on his way.

As England moved in for the kill, their fielding let them down. Geraint Jones put down Lee with a one-handed chance that might have been better left for Trescothick at slip. He fumbled a return, that was not easy to take, to miss a run out opportunity, and in a short time Pietersen was to make it six out of six in the series when it came to dropped catches.

Above
One of Geraint Jones wicket-keeping fumbles during the Trend Bridge Test.

Right
Strauss departs amid mounting tension after being dismissed by Warne to leave England on 57-3.

Before that, Jones made amends to a degree by stumping the free-hitting Warne off Giles, Harmison induced an edge by Kasprowicz and then bowled Tait to leave England a day and a session to score 129. A mere 129? No, all of 129.

Trescothick and Strauss went along very happily, taking 32 off the first five overs before Warne was introduced. Tresocthick was caught off Warne's first ball before Vaughan edged to slip and Strauss glanced to leg slip. When Bell played an unconvincing hook straight to long leg, England were 57 for four and the omens were no better than the nerves.

Flintoff and Pietersen appeared to have quietened the doubters with a stand of 46 in ten overs. Surely England would coast home now? Wrong again. From being in a position where a two-one series lead going into the final Test appeared a formality, the loss of Pietersen's wicket (caught behind off Lee) and then Flintoff (bowled Lee), meant that Australia could have taken a two-one lead themselves, ensuring retention of the Ashes that very afternoon.

That fear intensified when Geraint Jones went for glory by trying to hit Warne over the top, but succeeded only in presenting a simple catch to Kasprowicz. 116 for seven with Giles and Hoggard at the crease, and just Harmison and an injured Simon Jones in reserve. 13 runs needed.

Vaughan, asked after the match if he was confident that this pair had the right temperament and technique to withstand Warne and Lee and take England home, replied quite simply: "No." The crowd probably shared that sentiment, because every ball that failed to take a wicket was applauded and every run was cheered, even if it was a leg bye or a no ball.

With application and a steady nerve, to say nothing of courage against the rampaging Lee, the pair edged ever closer to the magic number. Belief returned to English ranks and drained from the Australians when Hoggard somehow found a cover dive off Lee that would have

Above
Euphoria on the England balcony after Giles and Hoggard seal a three-wicket win.

stood comparison with Wally Hammond in his pomp. With two needed, Giles got a full toss from Warne that he thumped into the leg side, only to hit Katich at short leg and a dot ball was the result. It only delayed the inevitable, for Warne bowled again on the leg side, Giles flicked it somewhere out towards mid-wicket and the batsmen just ran and ran. The ball may or may not have gone for four, but the completion of the second run that saw England over the line turned into an extended lap of honour. England had won by three wickets; the Ashes were very much alive; and the nation could let go a collective sigh of relief – if they had any breath left after holding it for so long.

Above Right
A jubilant Giles leaves the field after hitting the winning runs for England.

Right
England captain Vaughan shakes hands with Lee as the beaten Australians leave the field.

Red Stripe
vodafone
Brit Insurance
FRIENDS PROVIDENT
telegraph.co.uk
TOYOTA Avensis
FULLER'S LONDON PRIDE

Chapter Five

The Oval

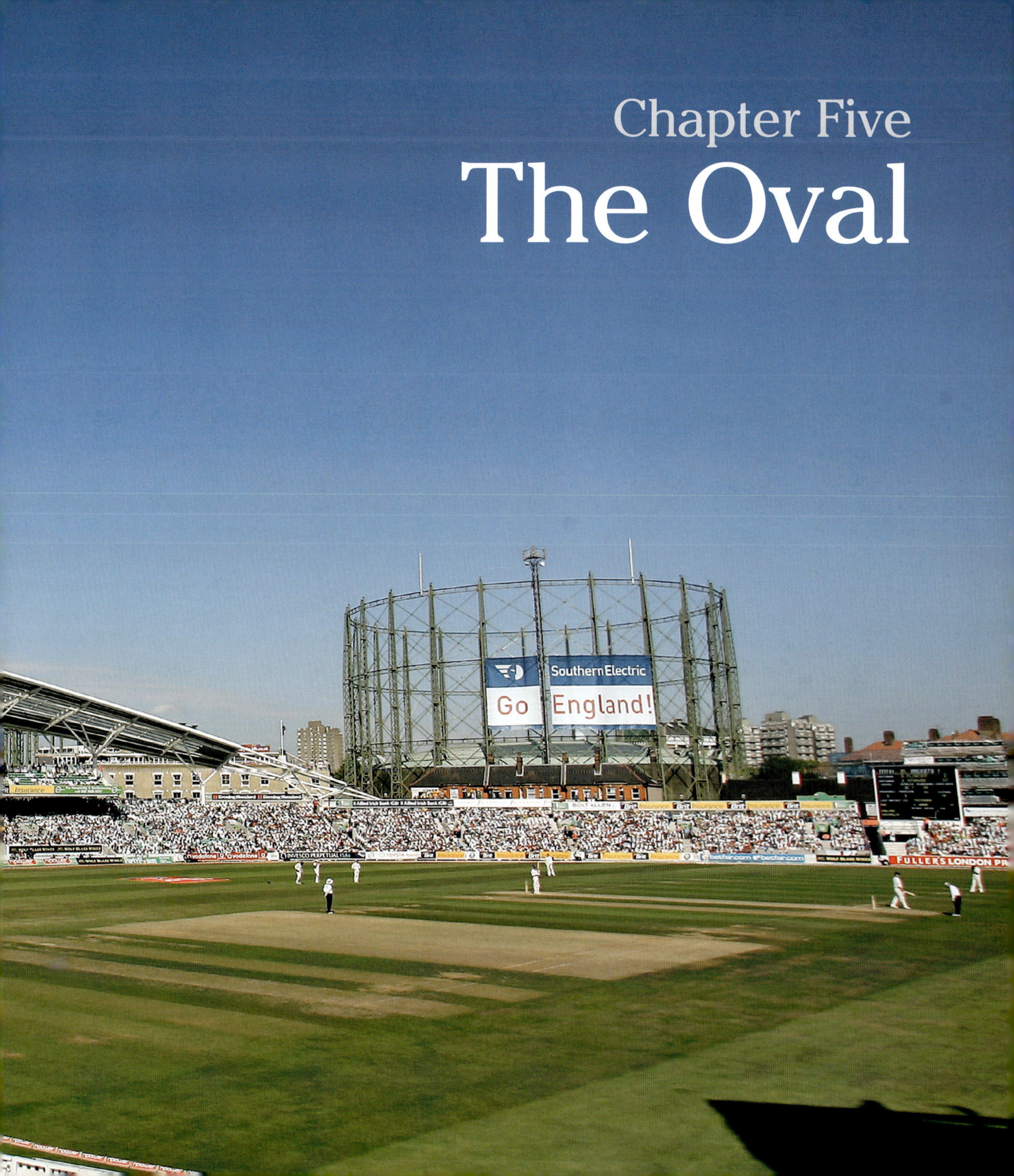

Left
The rivals: captains Michael Vaughan and Ricky Ponting ahead of the crucial final Test.

Below
Trescothick turns for the pavilion after being caught by Hayden at slip off Warne.

FOR the third time in succession, Michael Vaughan won a crucial toss and chose to bat on a sand-coloured Oval belter. But unlike at Edgbaston, Old Trafford and Trent Bridge, England failed to pass the 400 mark. Although Marcus Trescothick again gave them a rousing start, the Somerset left-hander was caught at slip by Matthew Hayden when he had made 43, becoming the first of three wickets to fall to Shane Warne before lunch. When, you may ask, did any Australian leg spinner last do that on day one of a Test match?

Perhaps the nerves of the occasion had got to Vaughan, who pulled loosely to be caught by Michael

Clarke at mid-wicket. Ian Bell was plumb lbw for a duck and worse followed after the interval when Kevin Pietersen, losing patience after being tied down by his Hampshire teammate, was bowled playing crookedly across the line.

Could Andrew Flintoff rise to yet another Ashes occasion? Happily for England, the answer proved affirmative as he shared a partnership of 143 for the fifth wicket with Andrew Strauss that put their team back on track. But with hopes rising of another imposing total Glenn McGrath, again restored to the Australian side after an elbow injury, induced an edge from Flintoff (72), which flew low to Warne at slip. Paul Collingwood was unlucky to be given out lbw as he played a shot to a

Below
An ungainly shot is Kevin Pietersen's downfall, bowled by Warne for 14.

delivery from Shaun Tait that was destined to pass his off stump. After reaching his second century of the series Strauss fell shortly before the close, caught by Simon Katich via bat and pad off Warne.

Hopes were high at the start of day two that Geraint Jones could combine with Ashley Giles to make a substantial improvement to England's overnight 319 for seven. In the event, the ninth ball of the morning from Brett Lee trimmed Jones' off stump straight after a drive to the cover boundary. So it was left to Ashley Giles, whose batting is still improving, and the tail to nudge and nurdle England on. Matthew Hoggard, without in the least suggesting permanence, kept Giles company while another 20 were added. Giles was fortunate to survive an appeal for a caught behind off McGrath that almost reduced the great fast bowler to apoplexy when umpire Rudi Koertzen turned it down. McGrath could not even bring himself to collect his cap at the end of the over.

Left
Strauss celebrates the crucial century which anchored England's first innings.

Above
McGrath cannot believe his luck after an unsuccessful appeal against Giles.

Hoggard was caught by Damien Martyn at extra cover in McGrath's next over, but Stephen Harmison contributed a swashbuckling, run-a-ball 20, with four boundaries, before Giles was eventually trapped in front by Warne, The incomparable Victorian ended with six for 122, and England had been dismissed for 373.

While Justin Langer and Matthew Hayden were putting on 185 for Australia's first wicket, England's total looked well below par. Langer needed the more good fortune; he was missed at slip by Trescothick off Collingwood when he had made 53, and was close to being out lbw to Giles shortly afterwards. The day ended

in some controversy, as storm clouds rolled in during the tea interval to plunge the ground into gloom. Offered the light on returning to the middle, the batsmen accepted. In the event the storm largely passed the ground by, leaving Australia vulnerable to claims that they were not doing everything possible to win the game. Rain did arrive to end the proceedings almost an hour later.

By the end of day three both Langer and Hayden had reached their first centuries of the series, Langer the 22nd of his Test career and Hayden his 21st. Shorn of the injured Simon Jones, the England attack was disciplined but temporarily toothless on a flat track. Langer, who also passed 7,000 Test runs during his innings, played on to his stumps during a fast and furious over from Harmison. Ricky Ponting, who should have been given out off bat

Far Left
Bad light and rain hamper Australian hopes of squaring the series on day two.

Left
Umpires Rudi Koertzen and Billy Bowden make one of several light checks as play is delayed.

Right
Aggressive intent: Langer hits one of two sixes in Giles' first over.

Far Right
Ponting reviews his own dismissal on the big screen after being caught by Strauss off Flintoff.

and pad when he was on 13, was surprised by a sharply lifting delivery from Flintoff that he could only fend to the diving Strauss at gully. But by the close Australia, on 277 for two, were aiming at a big first innings lead before setting Warne on England on the final day.

The script turned out to be entirely different, thanks to the bowling heroics of – guess who? On a gloomy fourth day, Flintoff bowled unchanged from the start until Australia were dismissed shortly after lunch, their last seven wickets falling for just 44 runs in 90 balls. Martyn went first in Flintoff's second over, cramped for room as he pulled a short ball to square leg where Collingwood held a straightforward catch.

Left
More joy for England and Hoggard after he traps Gilchrist lbw.

After England had taken the new ball, the batsmen were again offered the light but in Australia's anxiety to win, it was declined. With Hayden and Clarke trying to accelerate, Flintoff of all people, who may have had trouble picking the ball up in the gloom, missed Clarke at slip off Hoggard. Hayden went next; palpably lbw to a seaming delivery from Flintoff, and Katich followed in like manner just two overs later to a ball that would have hit his leg stump. Adam Gilchrist began with his characteristically bustling aggression, but to a tumultuous roar from the capacity Oval crowd, he became the third lbw victim of the session, pinned by a Hoggard inswinger as he hit across the line.

Clarke was again missed after the lunch interval, Jones diving one-handed in front of first slip in a manner that does not yet inspire confidence. Like most of his missed chances it mercifully turned out not to matter greatly; Clarke was almost immediately trapped lbw by Hoggard. An aerial pull off Flintoff from Warne was held at the second attempt by England's captain at long-on

Above
Flintoff celebrates after trapping Katich lbw for just a single.

Right
Flintoff and Hoggard salute the crowd after responding to the instruction on the gas holder.

and McGrath was taken in the slips off Hoggard, who finished the innings by having Lee caught at deep midwicket by Giles.

Flintoff finished with five for 78 from 34 overs, while Hoggard fully deserved his four for 97. Almost unbelievably given the score the previous evening, England had a slither of a lead with Australia 367 all out. But it had only risen from six to eight when Strauss inside-edged Warne to short leg, falling to the leg spinner for the sixth time in the series. The light at this point seemed

Left
Vaughan gives England a positive start as they build on their small lead.

barely playable, prompting much English sympathy for Strauss, but the Middlesex left-hander had done his team proud in the first innings.

Vaughan joined Trescothick to bat positively, particularly against McGrath, but no sooner had he played inside another spinning Warne delivery than the light was offered again, and this time to no one's surprise and to audible delight in the crowd, the batsmen accepted. Such enthusiasm for inactivity on the field is rare indeed, but after the repeated and extreme tension of this extraordinary series, many England supporters were beginning to feel that it no longer mattered not how the Ashes were won, provided the deed was sealed. It left the prospect of another final day cliffhanger, with brighter conditions forecast.

So it proved as the series, appropriately enough given its sensational nature, reached its last morning undecided. Despite a flowing start from Vaughan,

England were soon in trouble, at the hands not of Warne but his illustrious teammate. Vaughan was brilliantly caught by Gilchrist, whose one-handed effort off a seaming delivery from McGrath held a lesson for his English counterpart. The next ball, a hapless Ian Bell, for whom this series perhaps came a moment too soon, completed a pair when Warne held him at first slip.

The high drama continued as the hat-trick ball flew off Kevin Pietersen into the slips and prompted a raucous, unanimous appeal. Umpire Billy Bowden correctly ruled that it had come off Pietersen's shoulder, but he was then missed off Warne, a slip chance to Hayden made harder by a deflection from Gilchrist's glove. And in a near-perfect rubber blighted by a plethora of missed chances

Below
Golden duck – Bell completes a pair, edging a perfect McGrath delivery to Warne at slip.

Left
Close call – Warne looks on as Pietersen narrowly avoids being run out.

on either side, perhaps the most memorable error followed when Warne himself, again at first slip, dropped a fairly straightforward chance, off Pietersen with McGrath bowling, when the batsman had made 15.

Even so, as Warne lured Flintoff into driving him a return catch, Australia were scenting the kill as they have so often done in recent years, and once again the Ashes series had reached a blazing passage. Lee, perhaps fired up by the missed chances, produced an over of visceral pace in which a delivery close to 95mph crashed into Pietersen's ribcage. He went down and needed attention from the England physiotherapist Kirk Russell, but was not as badly hurt as first appeared. He later revealed that far from requiring attention to an injury, he was simply ensuring that, with the clock ticking round towards 12.30, he would deprive Warne of the opportunity to bowl another over before lunch.

When the players did indeed troop off at the end of the over, England were 127 for five and with 73 overs remaining, Australia undoubted favourites to win. The best hope for home supporters was simply that in a series where prediction had become a mug's game, another twist in the tail was possible in the last two sessions. Distracted people walked around aimlessly, unable to find the slightest relaxation from the matter in hand. Appetites for food had diminished, while text messages and mobile phone calls were exchanged in numbers that the network

Above
English anxiety grows as a distraught Flintoff is caught and bowled by Warne.

Right
Stand and deliver: one of many ferocious shots played by Pietersen during his defiant 158.

periodically failed to sustain. England's chairman of selectors David Graveney had become unable to watch during the morning session; he had withdrawn to listen to commentary on his car radio.

Over lunch though, Pietersen reached a decision about his approach on the resumption. He expected Lee

to continue propelling his high-velocity missiles, and concluded: "It's him or me." In the event, Lee's next three overs disappeared for 37 runs in a gladiatorial exchange that was to prove the turning point of the day. The roars from the crowd that greeted Pietersen's counter-attack, fuelled by tremendous physical strength matched by his own self-belief, made the Oval sound much as a Roman amphitheatre might have done centuries ago, as the real life gladiators of the time crossed their swords in a fight to the death.

Pietersen is known to be a vulnerable starter who bats with destructive power once he is in. One Lee delivery was swatted for six almost off the peak of his helmet; it was one of no less than seven times he was to clear the boundary. At the other end Collingwood did no less than was required of him for over an hour, defending stoutly while Pietersen wrought havoc.

Still, though, England were not safe. Just after hitting his first boundary, Collingwood was caught by Ponting at silly mid-on, and Warne now had ten wickets in the match. 186 for six, and for the first time in the day Ponting handed the ball to Shaun Tait. Pietersen took a brace of offside boundaries from the first two deliveries, but Jones, on just one, got a reverse swinging delivery in the same over which kept low and cannoned into the base of his off stump.

Could Giles, who had shown his customary tenacity in the first innings, produce a substantially larger chunk of the same? He began much as Collingwood had, defending stoutly and seeking sharp singles with such alacrity

Left
Pietersen unleashes another powerful pull as he blazes England towards Ashes glory.

Below
Magic moment – Pietersen celebrates a maiden Test century that could not have been more timely.

Right
With England assured of regaining the Ashes, Giles celebrates his vital half century.

Below Right
They think it's all over – and so does an exhausted Shane Warne.

that for a time he seemed to have more of the strike than Pietersen, whose hundred when he reached it, with a classic drive through extra cover, was greeted by one of the biggest roars of the day. England reached tea on 221 for seven, and the tension, with a bowler of Warne's class quite capable of finishing the innings with a hat-trick, remained high.

But as the two continued in the same vein afterwards, the equation between the runs needed by Australia and the remaining overs was shifting, almost imperceptibly but inexorably, in England's favour. Giles mixed watchful defence with the occasional booming boundary, while Pietersen entertained a rapturous crowd with a further dazzling array of strokeplay. Little landmarks were passed. When England reached 280, it was clear that Australia would need to go at more than eight an over to have any chance of victory. 299 signalled the hundred partnership, and thereafter increasing English confidence that the Ashes were coming home became euphoric certainty.

Australia took the new ball knowing it was too late to affect the outcome, and Pietersen, on 158, was bowled by it to become McGrath's final Test victim in England. Giles reached his best (and doubtless most memorable) score in Test cricket of 59 before he was bowled by Warne, who dismissed Harmison to finish with 12 wickets in the match and a record 40 in the series. Nevertheless, a man who hates losing more than most was feeling the urn slip out of Australia's grasp for the first time in his career.

Frustratingly, the final act included an element of farce. With England bowled out for 335, Australia were left needing an impossible 342 for victory. After Warne and McGrath had led Australia off, the England team took the field to more massed cheering. But after just one over of Harmison the batsmen were offered the light and after some confused consideration decided to go off. The game should have ended there and then, but instead we were put through an anti-climactic 15 minutes with the umpires nowhere to be seen and the series hanging in a limbo that did it a woeful injustice. At last the umpires reappeared and lifted the bails to signal the end.

Appropriately, the presentation was attended by the doyen of cricket commentators, Richie Benaud, who had just completed his final stint of commentary in England. Kevin Pietersen was named man of the match, Andrew Flintoff and Shane Warne the respective England and Australia players of the series, while Flintoff scooped the accolade of overall player of the series. After seven weeks of almost unbelievable tension, the champagne could mix with the

Above Left
Rooftop roar – England supporters cheer their team's triumph from every vantage point.

Left
Final act – after a quarter of an hour's confusion, the umpires finally draw stumps to end the match.

Above
Vintage moment – champagne to celebrate England achievement in winning an epic series.

Right
Michael Vaughan kisses the replica of the Ashes urn presented to him at the end of the match.

Far Right
An overjoyed Kevin Pietersen displays his man-of-the-match memorabilia.

confetti and those 23,000 souls at the Oval could know that they were part of a wonderful piece of cricketing history. The Ashes were back home after a gap of 16 years, and cricket had captivated the nation.

Celebrations

WHEN it became known that the England and Wales Cricket Board had provisionally booked Trafalgar Square as the destination for an open-top bus parade should England win back the Ashes, there was a certain amount of tutting, amid claims that it was tempting fate and references to hatching eggs. As it turned out, it was an inspired piece of planning.

Those who claimed that cricket's popularity could not be measured by attendances at county matches, and that there was a deep well of affection for the game waiting to be tapped, were totally vindicated. There would have been nothing worse than a parade watched by a few dozen people, or the players being presented to a couple of hundred followers in Trafalgar Square. Nobody need

Below
England players acknowledge the cheers of thousands of supporters as their open-top bus approaches Trafalgar Square.

Right
The England women's team had as much to celebrate after winning their version of the Ashes for the first time in 42 years.

have had any fears. England had not won the World Cup, they had not gained first place in the International Cricket Council's ranking table. But they had won back the Ashes after a ridiculously long period and the nation was ready to celebrate.

Thousands upon thousand turned out to give their full-throated approval to the England players as they were borne through streets thronged by the cheering masses. These people had left desks, they had travelled from far and wide, they had missed school, they had cried off sick from work. Only a few were lucky enough to be at the Oval the day before, but there was no apparent limit to the number who filled the route to Trafalgar Square and who took every vantage point to see their heroes and yell their congratulations.

Heroines too, for another bus was carrying the England Women's team, who had won their own version of the Ashes by beating Australia one-nil in the two-match series. It was the first time in 42 years that they had managed to claim their Ashes success, so there was every reason for them to join in the general euphoria and festive occasion.

Trafalgar Square was a sea of red and white. The crowds cheered and waved their flags of St. George. They sang "Jerusalem" with passion and fervour. They even excused, or perhaps encouraged, those members of the England team who had obviously not stopped celebrating from the moment the bails were removed at the Oval to signal that the long wait was over.

Asked just before the start of the Ashes series what the result would be, England's chairman of selectors David Graveney predicted a two-one win for his team. Although he was not in the majority, there was general agreement that the two sides were much better matched than

Left
Michael Vaughan and Kevin Pietersen display the Ashes urn, with the help of the Flintoffs, father and daughter.

Below
England's chairman of selectors David Graveney, who correctly predicted the 2-1 result before the series began.

Right
Talking tactics – Michael Vaughan and Duncan Fletcher consider the options before the final Test at the Oval.

before, and that the series should be closer than for many years. There was also a widely-held view that with Australia ageing and England youthful, England might have a better chance of wresting the urn back down under in 2006-07 than in England in 2005.

After Lord's, Graveney's prediction looked questionable. Not so after Edgbaston, which was in so many ways they key match of the rubber. From that moment on, England harried Australia as the men in baggy green have rarely been harried for more than a decade. And because Australia were used to being the bullies, they lacked the mental agility to hit back effectively. At times at Old Trafford they were run ragged in a game which, but for the rain on the third day, England would surely have won comfortably.

This burgeoning English confidence, this youthful uncertainty that comes with knowing you are improving but being unsure quite how heady are the heights you can reach, was glorious to witness. Perhaps it was personified most clearly by Freddie Flintoff, who in a team where every individual was repeatedly prepared to stand up and be counted, had the strength, the all-round talent and the lionhearted will to shine brightest of them all. "Super Fred" they chanted at the Oval. They were putting it mildly.

Just as Australia have done so effectively over the years, England had plans for how to deal with every opposition batsman, and the bowlers were disciplined enough to stick to them. As for England's batsmen, they too reaped the rewards of planning and hard work. And England, coached wisely and quietly by Duncan Fletcher, were led impeccably by Vaughan, constantly alert and looking for positive adjustments on the field, relaxed and good-humoured in dealing with the media off it.

Vaughan's captaincy contrasted with that of Ponting, who let himself down with his foul-mouthed outburst after being run out by the substitute, Gary Pratt, at Trent Bridge. Sometimes it appeared that Ponting was almost captaining by committee, although he lacked the bowling options that Vaughan possessed for the greater part of the series. As is usually the case when a great team grows old, it is difficult to know how quickly to ring the changes. Unlike England, it is now Australia who have most of the selection questions to answer. And sympathy is due in abundance to Warne, still the best bowler on either side.

WINNING THE ASHES

He took no less than 40 wickets, a record for a five-match Ashes series, yet like his great companion-in-arms, Glenn McGrath, was in a losing Ashes team for the first time.

Other, fantastic moments remain in the mind. Harmison's bouncing message to Ponting at Lord's that left the Australian captain needing stitches in his cheek, the snake-like Warne delivery that bowled Strauss at Edgbaston, Flintoff's six into the pavilion there, Strauss's catch to dismiss Gilchrist at Trent Bridge, and Pietersen's thrilling counter-attack at the Oval. But what mattered most about this series, perhaps even more than the result, was the spirit in which it was played. The one image to hold in the mind, and maybe to hang up on the wall in every sports hall in every school and college in the country, was that of Flintoff walking up to the devastated Lee, whose resolute batting had so nearly enabled Australia to steal the match, to console him at the moment of England's Edgbaston euphoria.

All these memories were fresh in the minds of the cheering thousands in Trafalgar Square. The words "fresh" and "minds" could not be joined when it came to most of the players, who found varying degrees of difficulty in moving from the bus to the stage to be introduced to the crowds as the men who had brought the Ashes back to home. They went on to a reception in Downing Street and then to Lord's to return the Ashes formally to the MCC – despite the fact that, of course, they had never physically been away.

Left
Ricky Ponting wipes off some of the blood after being hit by a ball from Stephen Harmison on day one at Lord's.

Above
Confetti rains down on Trafalgar Square as thousands of England supporters join in the celebrations.

Right
Grandstand view – 200 years after Trafalgar, can Admiral Lord Nelson ever have overseen anything like this?

Then it was on to lead the rest of their cricketing lives. It will be hard for them to return to normal, even when the cheering eventually dies down, because whatever else happens, these will be the men who brought the Ashes back to England in 2005. In the euphoria, the part played by the Australians should not be forgotten. It takes two sides to produce a great sporting contest, and what was seen at Lord's, Edgbaston, Old Trafford, Trent Bridge and the Oval in the summer of 2005 can be counted among the very greatest of sporting contests.

Scorecards

England v Australia – 1st Test at Lord's (21, 22, 23, 24 July 2005)

Australia 1st innings

JL Langer	c Harmison	b Flintoff	40
ML Hayden		b Hoggard	12
*RT Ponting	c Strauss	b Harmison	9
DR Martyn	c GO Jones	b SP Jones	2
MJ Clarke	lbw	b SP Jones	11
SM Katich	c GO Jones	b Harmison	27
+AC Gilchrist	c GO Jones	b Flintoff	26
SK Warne		b Harmison	28
B Lee	c GO Jones	b Harmison	3
JN Gillespie	lbw	b Harmison	1
GD McGrath	not out		10
Extras	(b 5, lb 4, w 1, nb 11)		21
Total	**(all out, 40.2 overs, 209 mins)**		**190**

FoW: 1-35 (Hayden, 7.6 ov), 2-55 (Ponting, 12.5 ov), 3-66 (Langer, 14.4 ov), 4-66 (Martyn, 15.1 ov), 5-87 (Clarke, 21.5 ov), 6-126 (Gilchrist, 28.3 ov), 7-175 (Warne, 36.1 ov), 8-178 (Katich, 36.3 ov), 9-178 (Lee, 38.4 ov), 10-190 (Gillespie, 40.2 ov).

Bowling	O	M	R	W	
Harmison	11.2	0	43	5	
Hoggard	8	0	40	1	(2nb)
Flintoff	11	2	50	2	(9nb)
SP Jones	10	0	48	2	(1w)

England 1st innings

ME Trescothick	c Langer	b McGrath	4
AJ Strauss	c Warne	b McGrath	2
*MP Vaughan		b McGrath	3
IR Bell		b McGrath	6
KP Pietersen	c Martyn	b Warne	57
A Flintoff		b McGrath	0
+GO Jones	c Gilchrist	b Lee	30
AF Giles	c Gilchrist	b Lee	11
MJ Hoggard	c Hayden	b Warne	0
SJ Harmison	c Martyn	b Lee	11
SP Jones	not out		20
Extras	(b 1, lb 5, nb 5)		11
Total	**(all out, 48.1 overs, 227 mins)**		**155**

FoW: 1-10 (Trescothick, 6.1 ov), 2-11 (Strauss, 6.5 ov), 3-18 (Vaughan, 12.2 ov), 4-19 (Bell, 14.3 ov), 5-21 (Flintoff, 16.1 ov), 6-79 (GO Jones, 34.1 ov), 7-92 (Giles, 36.6 ov), 8-101 (Hoggard, 41.4 ov), 9-122 (Pietersen, 43.4 ov), 10-155 (Harmison, 48.1 ov).

Bowling	O	M	R	W	
McGrath	18	5	53	5	
Lee	15.1	5	47	3	(4nb)
Gillespie	8	1	30	0	(1nb)
Warne	7	2	19	2	

Australia 2nd innings

JL Langer	run out (Pietersen)		6
ML Hayden	b Flintoff		34
*RT Ponting	c sub (Hildreth)	b Hoggard	42
DR Martyn	lbw	b Harmison	65
MJ Clarke		b Hoggard	91
SM Katich	c SP Jones	b Harmison	67
+AC Gilchrist		b Flintoff	10
SK Warne	c Giles	b Harmison	2
B Lee	run out (Giles)		8
JN Gillespie		b SP Jones	13
GD McGrath	not out		20
Extras	(b 10, lb 8, nb 8)		26
Total	**(all out, 100.4 overs, 457 mins)**		**384**

FoW: 1-18 (Langer, 5.3 ov), 2-54 (Hayden, 14.4 ov), 3-100 (Ponting, 27.3 ov), 4-255 (Clarke, 61.6 ov), 5-255 (Martyn, 62.1 ov), 6-274 (Gilchrist, 67.2 ov), 7-279 (Warne, 70.2 ov), 8-289 (Lee, 74.1 ov), 9-341 (Gillespie, 89.6 ov), 10-384 (Katich, 100.4 ov).

Bowling	O	M	R	W	
Harmison	27.4	6	54	3	
Hoggard	16	1	56	2	(2nb)
Flintoff	27	4	123	2	(5nb)
SP Jones	18	1	69	1	(1nb)
Giles	11	1	56	0	
Bell	1	0	8	0	

England 2nd innings

ME Trescothick	c Hayden	b Warne	44
AJ Strauss	c & b Lee		37
*MP Vaughan		b Lee	4
IR Bell	lbw	b Warne	8
KP Pietersen	not out		64
A Flintoff	c Gilchrist	b Warne	3
+GO Jones	c Gillespie	b McGrath	6
AF Giles	c Hayden	b McGrath	0
MJ Hoggard	lbw	b McGrath	0
SJ Harmison	lbw	b Warne	0
SP Jones	c Warne	b McGrath	0
Extras	(b 6, lb 5, nb 3)		14
Total	**(all out, 58.1 overs, 268 mins)**		**180**

FoW: 1-80 (Strauss, 26.3 ov), 2-96 (Trescothick, 29.2 ov), 3-104 (Bell, 33.1 ov), 4-112 (Vaughan, 36.2 ov), 5-119 (Flintoff, 39.3 ov), 6-158 (GO Jones, 50.3 ov), 7-158 (Giles, 50.5 ov), 8-164 (Hoggard, 54.6 ov), 9-167 (Harmison, 55.3 ov), 10-180 (SP Jones, 58.1 ov).

Bowling	O	M	R	W	
McGrath	17.1	2	29	4	
Lee	15	3	58	2	(1nb)
Gillespie	6	0	18	0	(2nb)
Warne	20	2	64	4	

Result: Australia won by 239 runs **Toss:** Australia **Umpires:** Aleem Dar (Pakistan) and RE Koertzen (South Africa) **TV Umpire:** MR Benson **Match Referee:** RS Madugalle (Sri Lanka) **Man of the Match:** GD McGrath

England v Australia – 2nd Test at Edgbaston (4, 5, 6, 7 August 2005)

England 1st innings

ME Trescothick	c Gilchrist	b Kasprowicz	90
AJ Strauss		b Warne	48
*MP Vaughan	c Lee	b Gillespie	24
IR Bell	c Gilchrist	b Kasprowicz	6
KP Pietersen	c Katich	b Lee	71
A Flintoff	c Gilchrist	b Gillespie	68
+GO Jones	c Gilchrist	b Kasprowicz	1
AF Giles	lbw	b Warne	23
MJ Hoggard	lbw	b Warne	16
SJ Harmison		b Warne	17
SP Jones	not out		19
Extras	(lb 9, w 1, nb 14)		24
Total	**(all out, 79.2 overs, 356 mins)**		**407**

FoW: 1-112 (Strauss, 25.3 ov), 2-164 (Trescothick, 32.3 ov), 3-170 (Bell, 32.6 ov), 4-187 (Vaughan, 36.6 ov), 5-290 (Flintoff, 54.3 ov), 6-293 (GO Jones, 57.4 ov), 7-342 (Giles, 65.1 ov), 8-348 (Pietersen, 66.3 ov), 9-375 (Harmison, 69.4 ov), 10-407 (Hoggard, 79.2 ov).

Bowling	O	M	R	W	
Lee	17	1	111	1	(3nb, 1w)
Gillespie	22	3	91	2	(3nb)
Kasprowicz	15	3	80	3	(8nb)
Warne	25.2	4	116	4	

Australia 1st innings

JL Langer	lbw	b SP Jones	82
ML Hayden	c Strauss	b Hoggard	0
*RT Ponting	c Vaughan	b Giles	61
DR Martyn	run out (Vaughan)		20
MJ Clarke	c GO Jones	b Giles	40
SM Katich	c GO Jones	b Flintoff	4
+AC Gilchrist	not out		49
SK Warne		b Giles	8
B Lee	c Flintoff	b SP Jones	6
JN Gillespie	lbw	b Flintoff	7
MS Kasprowicz	lbw	b Flintoff	0
Extras	(b 13, lb 7, w 1, nb 10)		31
Total	**(all out, 76 overs, 346 mins)**		**308**

FoW: 1-0 (Hayden, 1.1 ov), 2-88 (Ponting, 19.5 ov), 3-118 (Martyn, 24.5 ov), 4-194 (Clarke, 44.2 ov), 5-208 (Katich, 49.4 ov), 6-262 (Langer, 61.3 ov), 7-273 (Warne, 64.5 ov), 8-282 (Lee, 67.1 ov), 9-308 (Gillespie, 75.5 ov), 10-308 (Kasprowicz, 75.6 ov).

Bowling	O	M	R	W	
Harmison	11	1	48	0	(2nb)
Hoggard	8	0	41	1	(4nb)
SP Jones	16	2	69	2	(1nb, 1w)
Flintoff	15	1	52	3	(3nb)
Giles	26	2	78	3	

England 2nd innings

ME Trescothick	c Gilchrist	b Lee	21
AJ Strauss		b Warne	6
MJ Hoggard	c Hayden	b Lee	1
*MP Vaughan		b Lee	1
IR Bell	c Gilchrist	b Warne	21
KP Pietersen	c Gilchrist	b Warne	20
A Flintoff		b Warne	73
+GO Jones	c Ponting	b Lee	9
AF Giles	c Hayden	b Warne	8
SJ Harmison	c Ponting	b Warne	0
SP Jones	not out		12
Extras	(lb 1, nb 9)		10
Total	**(all out, 52.1 overs, 249 mins)**		**182**

FoW: 1-25 (Strauss, 6.2 ov), 2-27 (Trescothick, 11.2 ov), 3-29 (Vaughan, 11.5 ov), 4-31 (Hoggard, 13.5 ov), 5-72 (Pietersen, 24.6 ov), 6-75 (Bell, 26.5 ov), 7-101 (GO Jones, 33.6 ov), 8-131 (Giles, 44.3 ov), 9-131 (Harmison, 44.4 ov), 10-182 (Flintoff, 52.1 ov).

Bowling	O	M	R	W	
Lee	18	1	82	4	(5nb)
Gillespie	8	0	24	0	(1nb)
Kasprowicz	3	0	29	0	(3nb)
Warne	23.1	7	46	6	

Australia 2nd innings

JL Langer		b Flintoff	28
ML Hayden	c Trescothick	b SP Jones	31
*RT Ponting	c GO Jones	b Flintoff	0
DR Martyn	c Bell	b Hoggard	28
MJ Clarke		b Harmison	30
SM Katich	c Trescothick	b Giles	16
+AC Gilchrist	c Flintoff	b Giles	1
JN Gillespie	lbw	b Flintoff	0
SK Warne	hit wicket	b Flintoff	42
B Lee	not out		43
MS Kasprowicz	c GO Jones	b Harmison	20
Extras	(b 13, lb 8, w 1, nb 18)		40
Total	**(all out, 64.3 overs, 307 mins)**		**279**

FoW: 1-47 (Langer, 12.2 ov), 2-48 (Ponting, 12.6 ov), 3-82 (Hayden, 22.5 ov), 4-107 (Martyn, 26.1 ov), 5-134 (Katich, 31.6 ov), 6-136 (Gilchrist, 33.5 ov), 7-137 (Gillespie, 34.2 ov), 8-175 (Clarke, 43.4 ov), 9-220 (Warne, 52.1 ov), 10-279 (Kasprowicz, 64.3 ov).

Bowling	O	M	R	W	
Harmison	17.3	3	62	2	(1nb, 1w)
Hoggard	5	0	26	1	
Giles	15	3	68	2	
Flintoff	22	3	79	4	(13nb)
SP Jones	5	1	23	1	

Result: England won by 2 runs **Toss:** Australia **Umpires:** BF Bowden (New Zealand) and RE Koertzen (South Africa) **TV Umpire:** JW Lloyds **Match Referee:** RS Madugalle (Sri Lanka) **Man of the Match:** A Flintoff

England v Australia – 3rd Test at Old Trafford (11, 12, 13, 14, 15 August 2005)

England 1st innings

ME Trescothick	c Gilchrist	b Warne	63
AJ Strauss		b Lee	6
*MP Vaughan	c McGrath	b Katich	166
IR Bell	c Gilchrist	b Lee	59
KP Pietersen	c sub (BJ Hodge)	b Lee	21
MJ Hoggard		b Lee	4
A Flintoff	c Langer	b Warne	46
+GO Jones		b Gillespie	42
AF Giles	c Hayden	b Warne	0
SJ Harmison	not out		10
SP Jones		b Warne	0
Extras	(b 4, lb 5, w 3, nb 15)		27
Total	**(all out, 113.2 overs, 503 mins)**		**444**

FoW: 1-26 (Strauss, 9.2 ov), 2-163 (Trescothick, 41.5 ov), 3-290 (Vaughan, 74.3 ov), 4-333 (Pietersen, 86.2 ov), 5-341 (Hoggard, 88.6 ov), 6-346 (Bell, 92.1 ov), 7-433 (Flintoff, 109.2 ov), 8-434 (GO Jones, 110.2 ov), 9-438 (Giles, 111.4 ov), 10-444 (SP Jones, 113.2 ov).

Bowling	O	M	R	W	
McGrath	25	6	86	0	(4nb)
Lee	27	6	100	4	(5nb, 2w)
Gillespie	19	2	114	1	(2nb, 1w)
Warne	33.2	5	99	4	(2nb)
Katich	9	1	36	1	

Australia 1st innings

JL Langer	c Bell	b Giles	31
ML Hayden	lbw	b Giles	34
*RT Ponting	c Bell	b SP Jones	7
DR Martyn		b Giles	20
SM Katich		b Flintoff	17
+AC Gilchrist	c GO Jones	b SP Jones	30
SK Warne	c Giles	b SP Jones	90
MJ Clarke	c Flintoff	b SP Jones	7
JN Gillespie	lbw	b SP Jones	26
B Lee	c Trescothick	b SP Jones	1
GD McGrath	not out		1
Extras	(b 8, lb 7, w 8, nb 15)		38
Total	**(all out, 84.5 overs, 393 mins)**		**302**

FoW: 1-58 (Langer, 15.5 ov), 2-73 (Ponting, 20.1 ov), 3-86 (Hayden, 23.3 ov), 4-119 (Katich, 32.1 ov), 5-133 (Martyn, 35.3 ov), 6-186 (Gilchrist, 48.1 ov), 7-201 (Clarke, 52.3 ov), 8-287 (Warne, 76.2 ov), 9-293 (Lee, 80.4 ov), 10-302 (Gillespie, 84.5 ov).

Bowling	O	M	R	W	
Harmison	10	0	47	0	(3nb)
Hoggard	6	2	22	0	
Flintoff	20	1	65	1	(8nb)
SP Jones	17.5	6	53	6	(1nb, 2w)
Giles	31	4	100	3	(1w)

England 2nd innings

ME Trescothick		b McGrath	41
AJ Strauss	c Martyn	b McGrath	106
*MP Vaughan	c sub (BJ Hodge)	b Lee	14
IR Bell	c Katich	b McGrath	65
KP Pietersen	lbw	b McGrath	0
A Flintoff		b McGrath	4
+GO Jones	not out		27
AF Giles	not out		0
Extras	(b 5, lb 3, w 1, nb 14)		23
Total	**(6 wkts dec, 61.5 overs, 288 mins)**		**280**

DNB: MJ Hoggard, SJ Harmison, SP Jones.

FoW: 1-64 (Trescothick, 15.3 ov), 2-97 (Vaughan, 25.4 ov), 3-224 (Strauss, 53.3 ov), 4-225 (Pietersen, 53.5 ov), 5-248 (Flintoff, 59.1 ov), 6-264 (Bell, 61.1 ov).

Bowling	O	M	R	W	
McGrath	20.5	1	115	5	(6nb, 1w)
Lee	12	0	60	1	(4nb)
Warne	25	3	74	0	
Gillespie	4	0	23	0	(4nb)

Australia 2nd innings

JL Langer	c GO Jones	b Hoggard	14
ML Hayden		b Flintoff	36
*RT Ponting	c GO Jones	b Harmison	156
DR Martyn	lbw	b Harmison	19
SM Katich	c Giles	b Flintoff	12
+AC Gilchrist	c Bell	b Flintoff	4
MJ Clarke		b SP Jones	39
JN Gillespie	lbw	b Hoggard	0
SK Warne	c GO Jones	b Flintoff	34
B Lee	not out		18
GD McGrath	not out		5
Extras	(b 5, lb 8, w 1, nb 20)		34
Total	**(9 wickets, 108 overs, 474 mins)**		**371**

FoW: 1-25 (Langer, 11.1 ov), 2-96 (Hayden, 29.4 ov), 3-129 (Martyn, 42.5 ov), 4-165 (Katich, 49.3 ov), 5-182 (Gilchrist, 57.4 ov), 6-263 (Clarke, 75.2 ov), 7-264 (Gillespie, 76.5 ov), 8-340 (Warne, 98.2 ov), 9-354 (Ponting, 103.6 ov).

Bowling	O	M	R	W	
Harmison	22	4	67	2	(4nb, 1w)
Hoggard	13	0	49	2	(6nb)
Giles	26	4	93	0	
Vaughan	5	0	21	0	
Flintoff		25	6 71	4	(9nb)
SP Jones	17	3	57	1	

Result: Match Drawn **Toss:** England **Umpires:** BF Bowden (New Zealand) and SA Bucknor (West Indies) **TV Umpire:** NJ Llong **Match Referee:** RS Madugalle (Sri Lanka) **Man of the Match:** RT Ponting

England v Australia – 4th Test at Trent Bridge (25, 26, 27, 28 August 2005)

England 1st innings

ME Trescothick		b Tait	65
AJ Strauss	c Hayden	b Warne	35
*MP Vaughan	c Gilchrist	b Ponting	58
IR Bell	c Gilchrist	b Tait	3
KP Pietersen	c Gilchrist	b Lee	45
A Flintoff	lbw	b Tait	102
+GO Jones	c & b Kasprowicz		85
AF Giles	lbw	b Warne	15
MJ Hoggard	c Gilchrist	b Warne	10
SJ Harmison	st Gilchrist	b Warne	2
SP Jones	not out		15
Extras	(b 1, lb 15, w 1, nb 25)		42
Total	**(all out, 123.1 overs, 537 mins)**		**477**

FoW: 1-105 (Strauss, 21.4 ov), 2-137 (Trescothick, 30.5 ov), 3-146 (Bell, 34.1 ov), 4-213 (Vaughan, 55.2 ov), 5-241 (Pietersen, 64.1 ov), 6-418 (Flintoff, 103.2 ov), 7-450 (GO Jones, 112.5 ov), 8-450 (Giles, 113.1 ov), 9-454 (Harmison, 115.1 ov), 10-477 (Hoggard, 123.1 ov).

Bowling	O	M	R	W	
Lee	32	2	131	1	(8nb)
Kasprowicz	32	3	122	1	(13nb)
Tait	24	4	97	3	(4nb)
Warne	29.1	4	102	4	
Ponting	6	2	9	1	(1w)

Australia 1st innings

JL Langer	c Bell	b Hoggard	27
ML Hayden	lbw	b Hoggard	7
*RT Ponting	lbw	b SP Jones	1
DR Martyn	lbw	b Hoggard	1
MJ Clarke	lbw	b Harmison	36
SM Katich	c Strauss	b SP Jones	45
+AC Gilchrist	c Strauss	b Flintoff	27
SK Warne	c Bell	b SP Jones	0
B Lee	c Bell	b SP Jones	47
MS Kasprowicz		b SP Jones	5
SW Tait	not out	3	
Extras	(lb 2, w 1, nb 16)		19
Total	**(all out, 49.1 overs, 247 mins)**		**218**

FoW: 1-20 (Hayden, 9.3 ov), 2-21 (Ponting, 10.3 ov), 3-22 (Martyn, 11.1 ov), 4-58 (Langer, 19.3 ov), 5-99 (Clarke, 30.3 ov), 6-157 (Katich, 39.2 ov), 7-157 (Warne, 39.3 ov), 8-163 (Gilchrist, 42.2 ov), 9-175 (Kasprowicz, 43.2 ov), 10-218 (Lee, 49.1 ov).

Bowling	O	M	R	W	
Harmison	9	1	48	1	(3nb)
Hoggard	15	3	70	3	(4nb)
SP Jones	14.1	4	44	5	(1nb)
Flintoff	11	1	54	1	(8nb, 1w)

England 2nd innings

JL Langer	c Bell	b Giles	61
ML Hayden	c Giles	b Flintoff	26
*RT Ponting	run out (sub [GJ Pratt])		48
DR Martyn	c GO Jones	b Flintoff	13
MJ Clarke	c GO Jones	b Hoggard	56
SM Katich	lbw	b Harmison	59
+AC Gilchrist	lbw	b Hoggard	11
SK Warne	st GO Jones	b Giles	45
B Lee	not out		26
MS Kasprowicz	c GO Jones	b Harmison	19
SW Tait		b Harmison	4
Extras	(b 1, lb 4, nb 14)		19
Total	**(all out, 124 overs, 548 mins)**		**387**

FoW: 1-50 (Hayden, 13.4 ov), 2-129 (Langer, 33.6 ov), 3-155 (Ponting, 44.1 ov), 4-161 (Martyn, 46.1 ov), 5-261 (Clarke, 94.2 ov), 6-277 (Gilchrist, 98.5 ov), 7-314 (Katich, 107.3 ov), 8-342 (Warne, 112.3 ov), 9-373 (Kasprowicz, 119.2 ov), 10-387 (Tait, 123.6 ov).

Bowling	O	M	R	W	
Hoggard	27	7	72	2	(1nb)
SP Jones	4	0	15	0	
Harmison	30	5	93	3	(1nb)
Flintoff	29	4	83	2	(9nb)
Giles	28	3	107	2	
Bell	6	2	12	0	(3nb)

Australia 2nd innings

ME Trescothick	c Ponting	b Warne	27
AJ Strauss	c Clarke	b Warne	23
*MP Vaughan	c Hayden	b Warne	0
IR Bell	c Kasprowicz	b Lee	3
KP Pietersen	c Gilchrist	b Lee	23
A Flintoff		b Lee	26
+GO Jones	c Kasprowicz	b Warne	3
AF Giles	not out		7
MJ Hoggard	not out		8
Extras	(lb 4, nb 5)		9
Total	**(7 wickets, 31.5 overs, 168 mins)**		**129**

DNB: SJ Harmison, SP Jones.

FoW: 1-32 (Trescothick, 5.1 ov), 2-36 (Vaughan, 7.1 ov), 3-57 (Strauss, 13.5 ov), 4-57 (Bell, 14.1 ov), 5-103 (Pietersen, 24.1 ov), 6-111 (Flintoff, 26.4 ov), 7-116 (GO Jones, 27.6 ov).

Bowling	O	M	R	W	
Lee	12	0	51	3	(5nb)
Kasprowicz	2	0	19	0	
Warne	13.5	2	31	4	
Tait	4	0	24	0	

Result: England won by 3 wickets **Toss:** England **Umpires:** Aleem Dar (Pakistan) and SA Bucknor (West Indies) **TV Umpire:** MR Benson **Match Referee:** RS Madugalle (Sri Lanka) **Man of the Match:** A Flintoff

England v Australia – 5th Test at the Oval (8, 9, 10, 11, 12 September 2005)

England 1st innings

ME Trescothick	c Hayden	b Warne	43
AJ Strauss	c Katich	b Warne	129
*MP Vaughan	c Clarke	b Warne	11
IR Bell	lbw	b Warne	0
KP Pietersen		b Warne	14
A Flintoff	c Warne	b McGrath	72
PD Collingwood	lbw	b Tait	7
+GO Jones		b Lee	25
AF Giles	lbw	b Warne	32
MJ Hoggard	c Martyn	b McGrath	2
SJ Harmison	not out		20
Extras	(b 4, lb 6, w 1, nb 7)		18
Total	**(all out, 105.3 overs, 471 mins)**		**373**

FoW: 1-82 (Trescothick, 17.3 ov), 2-102 (Vaughan, 23.5 ov), 3-104 (Bell, 25.6 ov), 4-131 (Pietersen, 33.3 ov), 5-274 (Flintoff, 70.1 ov), 6-289 (Collingwood, 76.3 ov), 7-297 (Strauss, 79.4 ov), 8-325 (Jones, 89.3 ov), 9-345 (Hoggard, 100.2 ov), 10-373 (Giles, 105.3 ov).

Bowling	O	M	R	W	
McGrath	27	5	72	2	(1w)
Lee	23	3	94	1	(3nb)
Tait	15	1	61	1	(3nb)
Warne	37.3	5	122	6	
Katich	3	0	14	0	

Australia 1st innings

JL Langer		b Harmison	105
ML Hayden	lbw	b Flintoff	138
*RT Ponting	c Strauss	b Flintoff	35
DR Martyn	c Collingwood	b Flintoff	10
MJ Clarke	lbw	b Hoggard	25
SM Katich	lbw	b Flintoff	1
+AC Gilchrist	lbw	b Hoggard	23
SK Warne	c Vaughan	b Flintoff	0
B Lee	c Giles	b Hoggard	6
GD McGrath	c Strauss	b Hoggard	0
SW Tait	not out		1
Extras	(b 4, lb 8, w 2, nb 9)		23
Total	**(all out, 107.1 overs, 494 mins)**		**367**

FoW: 1-185 (Langer, 52.4 ov), 2-264 (Ponting, 72.2 ov), 3-281 (Martyn, 80.4 ov), 4-323 (Hayden, 92.3 ov), 5-329 (Katich, 94.6 ov), 6-356 (Gilchrist, 101.1 ov), 7-359 (Clarke, 103.3 ov), 8-363 (Warne, 104.5 ov), 9-363 (McGrath, 105.6 ov), 10-367 (Lee, 107.1 ov).

Bowling	O	M	R	W	
Harmison	22	2	87	1	(2nb, 2w)
Hoggard	24.1	2	97	4	(1nb)
Flintoff	34	10	78	5	(6nb)
Giles	23	1	76	0	
Collingwood	4	0	17	0	

England 2nd innings

ME Trescothick	lbw	b Warne	33
AJ Strauss	c Katich	b Warne	1
*MP Vaughan	c Gilchrist	b McGrath	45
IR Bell	c Warne	b McGrath	0
KP Pietersen		b McGrath	158
A Flintoff	c & b Warne		8
PD Collingwood	c Ponting	b Warne	10
+GO Jones		b Tait	1
AF Giles		b Warne	59
MJ Hoggard	not out		4
SJ Harmison	c Hayden	b Warne	0
Extras	(b 4, w 7, nb 5)		16
Total	**(all out, 91.3 overs, 432 mins)**		**335**

FoW: 1-2 (Strauss, 3.4 ov), 2-67 (Vaughan, 22.4 ov), 3-67 (Bell, 22.5 ov), 4-109 (Trescothick, 33.1 ov), 5-126 (Flintoff, 37.5 ov), 6-186 (Collingwood, 51.5 ov), 7-199 (Jones, 56.5 ov), 8-308 (Pietersen, 82.5 ov), 9-335 (Giles, 91.1 ov), 10-335 (Harmison, 91.3 ov).

Bowling	O	M	R	W	
McGrath	26	3	85	3	(1nb)
Lee	20	4	88	0	(4nb, 1w)
Warne	38.3	3	124	6	(1w)
Clarke	2	0	6	0	
Tait	5	0	28	1	(1w)

Australia 2nd innings

JL Langer	not out	0
ML Hayden	not out	0
Extras	(lb 4)	4
Total	**(0 wickets, 0.4 overs, 3 mins)**	**4**

DNB: *RT Ponting, DR Martyn, MJ Clarke, SM Katich, +AC Gilchrist, SK Warne, B Lee, GD McGrath, SW Tait.

Bowling	O	M	R	W
Harmison	0.4	0	0	0

Result: Match Drawn **Toss:** England **Umpires:** BF Bowden (New Zealand) and RE Koertzen (South Africa) **TV Umpire:** JW Lloyds **Match Referee:** RS Madugalle (Sri Lanka) **Man of the Match:** KP Pietersen

Players of the Series: A Flintoff and SK Warne

Images provided courtesy of:
Getty Images, 101 Bayham Street, London NW1 0AG

Additional photography:
Neil Harrington

Design, artwork and image research:
Kevin Gardner

Project Editors:
Jules Gammond, Tim Exell and Vanessa Gardner

Written by:
Ralph Dellor and Stephen Lamb

With special thanks to:
Frank Davis at The Lord's Taverners

クリスト：アンブレラ 日本ーアメリカ合衆国 1984－91
茨木、日本側

CHRISTO: THE UMBRELLAS JAPAN – USA 1984-91
IBARAKI, JAPAN SITE

MARCO LIVINGSTONE

OBJECTS FOR THE IDEAL HOME

The title of the Serpentine exhibition running concurrently with the Royal Academy Pop Art Show, Objects for the Ideal Home, *refers to Richard Hamilton's early Pop piece* Just what is it that makes today's homes so different, so appealing?. *Visually, this provides a summary of Pop art's fascination with consumerism, advertising and mass-production, sex and banality. The Serpentine show aimed to explore the continuing influence of the Pop movement on contemporary artists today and the similar concern with works based on the familiar and the domestic which are transformed into icons of everyday living. The metaphor of the department store was chosen to define the Serpentine's spaces, each room being given a title that alludes to the objects for sale: Fixtures and Fittings; Home Improvements; Originals and Replicas; Objets d'Art; Sign Systems. Brought together were 30 works by American and European artists of great stylistic diversity ranging from the modifications of fabricated objects by Rosemarie Trockel and Bertrand Lavier, the pristine sculptures of Julian Opie with their machine-like finish to the hilarity of Jeff Koons'* Winter Bears. *The following piece from the catalogue discusses Fixtures and Fittings:*

Tony Cragg, Zooid, *1991, steel and sandblasted porcelain, 93x37x30cm each (photo Stephen White)*

OVERLEAF: 'Objects for the Ideal Home', Serpentine Gallery, London, (clockwise) Allan McCollum, Perfect Vehicle no 676, *1989; Julian Opie,* M, *1988; Cady Noland,* Clip on Method, *1989; Edward Allington,* Curved Pediment, *1990; Michael Craig-Martin,* Untitled, *1991; Grenville Davey,* Button, *1988 (photo Stephen White)*

One of the challenges presented in the 1960s by Pop Art, in a reversal of Duchamp's invention of the ready-made half a century earlier, was to investigate the point at which a newly fabricated artefact almost ceases to declare itself as art by mimicking as closely as possible the appearance of an ordinary functional object. Given their concern with the things of everyday life, surprisingly little sculpture of this literal imitative sort emerged from the ranks of Pop artists. One can cite, for example, Andy Warhol's *Brillo Boxes* screenprinted on plywood boxes of the same size and colour as the supermarket cartons that they took as their model, and Richard Artschwager's formica furniture sculpture, stylised and plainly synthetic evocations of standard items deprived of their expected function. Pop's most assiduous fabricator of commonplace objects, Claes Oldenburg, worked only briefly in the early 1960s on a one-to-one scale in plaster replicas of food and items of clothing; in any case the exaggeratedly handmade look, impulsively applied paint and anthropomorphic qualities of these colourful plaster surrogates ruled out the possibility of even the most momentary confusion between art and life.

Since the late 1980s, however, there has been a proliferation of sculpture masquerading as ordinary objects. Some of these, such as the sinks, urinals, doors and playpens of the American Robert Gober, have plainly been made by hand. Others are more immaculately finished and suggestive of machine production, such as Artschwager's simulated furnishings or the architectural fittings produced by artists working in Britain, such as Michael Craig-Martin, Julian Opie and Grenville Davey, whether they are made by the artist himself or by specialist technicians following his or her instructions. The literalness and formal clarity of Minimalism, and the meanings invested in the object and in the gallery space itself by conceptual art, inform the much more extreme stance taken in the 1980s and 1990s by many of these object makers. The rather antiseptic quality of much of their immaculately finished work,

Robert Gober, Bent Door, *1988, wood, steel and enamel paint, 81x76x50cm*

furthermore, which makes even the depersonalised surfaces of Pop look almost quaintly handmade, also acknowledges the role now played by contemporary art as a valuable commodity in a multinational business and reflects the dominance of High-Tech taste in interior design for objects with clean lines and a precise machine-made look

Neither Minimalism nor conceptual art ever succeeded in overcoming public suspicion that they represented the artistic equivalent of the Emperor's new clothes: the furore attending the reception of Carl Andre's 'bricks' indicated a general unease about the apparent gulf between the profound meanings ascribed to contemporary art and their ever simpler visual form. In the late 1970s even David Hockney, only 20 years earlier the *enfant terrible* of contemporary British art, challenged an interviewer to justify why a Minimalist sculpture should be intrinsically more interesting to look at than a ventilator grill in the gallery floor. His questioner, a Tate Gallery curator, responded defensively by suggesting that the artist was adopting a Philistine attitude. Yet here we are, just a decade or so later, faced with the work of sculptors and painters who are defiantly producing art that dares to question its own identity as a sign for a different order of experience by exaggerating its resemblance to things we already know.

Many of these works take the form of fixtures and fittings; but other utilitarian objects, drained of their function, may as usefully serve as a reference point for investigations that are at once formal and social. The steady production by Allan McCollum of decoratively appealing *Perfect Vehicles,* vessels identical in their precisely symmetrical shape and uniformly smooth surface conceived in two sizes and an endless permutation of colours, calls to mind the processes of mass production and the importance ascribed to standards of excellence within industry. The customer may want to exercise choice, but also expects a certain standard. The example displayed here, in the larger of the two available sizes, is cast as a hollow concrete shell with the help of a team of assistants. Like all of McCollum's work, such as each of the *10,000 Individual Works* cast in plaster from different combinations of moulds made from ordinary objects, it is thus handmade and unique, while still reverberating with allusions to the identical machine-made products of the consumer culture that it serves to humanise.

Whatever the studio conditions of an artist working today, the safe assumption is that his or her wares will eventually be displayed in a clean, elegant, anonymous white box known as an art gallery or museum. Naturally, perhaps, many sculptors have thus come to focus on the relationship of their work to such settings by producing objects that are almost indistinguishable from architectural features. Our reading thus alternates between the virtual invisibility of these subtle intrusions, momentarily deflecting our attention onto the space as a whole, and a sudden realisation of their function in altering our perceptions of the environment. Edward Allington's *Curved Pediment,* for example, in being placed above a doorway, might at first pass unnoticed, but this reshaping in manganese zinc of a feature of classical architecture would inevitably transform the character of even the blandest modern interior.

Over the past few years Julian Opie has limited himself to the production of sculptures, so pristine and machine-made in appearance that they might have just left the factory, that deftly mimic the appearance of precisely such features of anonymous contemporary interiors: ventilation outlets, display cases, shelving and partitions. They make no visible concession to traditional sculptural norms. Indeed, seen outside a gallery context they might well be taken for granted as part of the furnishings, so convincing is their disguise. For that matter, were it not for their labelling and for the expectations engendered by the context, they might pass unnoticed even in the typical spaces of current commercial galleries, so standardised and sterile have these places become as showrooms for the latest commodities in international art. The transformation of these fixtures and fittings into art objects is effected by their presentation as such in the controlled circumstances of Spartan gallery interiors, focussing attention on their Minimalist formal properties and on their blatant lack of any utilitarian purpose. Context and intentionality, as conceptual artists had maintained in the late 1960s, become the vital elements in conveying their meaning.

Cecile Johnson, Eight Vases, *1990-91, clay, wood, paint, 132x178x32cm*

Michael Craig-Martin, who taught Opie at Goldsmiths' College of Art in London, is one of the senior figures working within such terms in British sculpture. From the late 1960s he used humble materials associated with carpentry (plywood and store-bought hinges) to produce simple forms that look like ordinary boxes but that have been deprived of their expected function because of the way in which the constituent elements have been interchanged. Consistently intrigued by the boundary between art and non-art and between one medium and another, in the past few years he has conceived works made to his specifications from venetian blinds. Although they can be described as paintings – in that they consist of a flat coloured surface fixed to the wall and take their geometric rigour from rules of Minimalist composition – they are actually three-dimensional objects, with colour intrinsic to the surface rather than added on. They are fixed in place in the same way as functional blinds, but if raised or opened they reveal only a blank expanse of wall.

Robert Gober's sculptures are conceived, like decoys: as things that catch us off guard by adopting a spurious form. *Bent Door,* like all these sculptures resembling familiar things, creates a momentary confusion between the art object and what it represents and in doing so helps ultimately to revitalise our appreciation of the artistic process by which it has been brought into being. Just as what most counts in a drawing is the way it has been done, rather than what it pictures, so in sculpture we are left with the material evidence of its medium and method of manufacture. Grenville Davey's painted steel *Button,* like an oversized prototype for a buzzer of the most ordinary kind, may well remind us that even the most prosaic objects that we encounter in our daily lives have been designed by someone and fabricated only as the last stage of visualisation; yet these sculptures, too, are presented as objects that have been stripped of their practical use so as to heighten our appreciation for their highly particularised presence as unique artefacts in their own right.

It is intrinsic to the meaning of most of these works that, however close their resemblance to real things, they have been made afresh, whether by the artist or by someone acting under his or her instructions. In certain cases, however, the distinction between elements made to order and others found ready-made is of less significance than the nature of the objects themselves. Davey, for instance, sometimes combines the two in a single work so that their origins are virtually indistinguishable. In the case of Cady Noland, the structure often looks made-to-measure although the fragments within it have clearly been found or bought specially for inclusion; the circumstances which brought each segment into being, however, do not make one more 'real' than another. The often disturbing impact of her work arises from the connotations of the things themselves. The objects on the metal pole of her *Clip on Method,* for example, include not only harmlessly handy implements such as a shoe-horn, but also devices signifying lonely sexuality (a dildo suspended from a chain) or self-defence (elements of a crooklock and fire extinguisher), pieces of wood, plastic or metal that seem useless in themselves, and even empty metal rings, all dangled in desultory fashion like charms on a bracelet.

The introspective tone and handmade quality of Cecile Johnson's work stands in striking contrast to these anxious adjuncts to modern urban life. Johnson's vases, pitchers, jars and other functional-

Haim Steinbach, Untitled (cabbage, pumpkin, cabbage no 1), *mixed media construction, 119x70x136cm*

looking objects have been re-shaped by hand in the same clay from which the actual things would be made, and then displayed on wall-mounted shelves that encourage them to be viewed frontally as still-lifes or friezes. The associations with museum cabinets, storage shelves or more domestic forms of display continue the metaphorical connection with prosaic functions, but again to heighten our perception of the status as sculpture of these forever empty containers. Each of her *Eight Vases* has been fitted together from a plausible combination of three standard elements, the subtleties of their design called to attention as a way of eliciting our contemplation.